PAINT YOURSELF HEALED

PAINT YOURSELF HEALED

Healed by God of Brain Cancer

E. Michal Gayer

Lightshine
Publishers

PAINT YOURSELF HEALED!
HEALED BY GOD OF BRAIN CANCER
Copyright © 2017 by E. Michal Gayer

ISBN 978-0-9654759-6-9

Published by
LIGHTSHINE PUBLISHERS
P.O. Box 225
Stuarts Draft, VA 24477

Cover and book formatting by Becky Marcum.

DEDICATED

To all who dare to believe in healing through Biblical principles.

To my parents Elizabeth and Steve Bahorik whose gift of love led me to Jesus Christ.

To my husband Bob whose love and strength vitalize me as we walk God's path together through the Valley of the Shadow of Death and beyond.

To my sons Robbyn, Brett and Bob and their families who bring me great joy and love as life companions.

To my brothers Stephen and Wesley Bahorik and their families who bring sustaining love and peace as fellow travelers in life's journey.

To all the men and women of God who stood with me through ministry and prayer contributing to my healing.

To all the medical professionals who ministered to me through medical knowledge and skill.

About the Author

E. Michal Gayer writes from a unique background of deep involvement in church ministry work after departing from a successful career as a Christian psychologist. Her education and training afford the exceptional combination of her having a well-developed understanding of human personality, character and relationships as well as a deep and rich grasp of Christian ministry work. She holds a Bachelor of Arts Degree from Juniata College, a Master of Arts Degree in Clinical Psychology from Wayne State University, and has pursued studies through Life Bible College and the Shenandoah Bible Institute. Professional licenses, which she has received during her lifetime, include Staff and District Ministerial Licenses from the Southeast District of the Church of the Foursquare Gospel, International Ministerial License with the International Church of the Foursquare Gospel, Psychologist License (PA) and Psychological Diagnostician License (MI). Michal is ordained as a minister of the Gospel and authorized to administer the ordinances of the Church by the International Church of the Foursquare Gospel.

Her ministry work includes teaching and preaching as well developing and administrating specialized Christian ministry and educational programs. These programs have focused mainly on the needs of individuals who are in need of healing. Michal is the Founding Director of the Healing Rooms of Augusta County, VA. She and her husband Robert are the Founding Directors of Lightshine Ministries International. They have ministered together in hundreds of churches across the United States of America preaching the healing Gospel of Jesus Christ and assisting churches in developing outreach programs for the sick. Other experiences she has had include having worked as a School Psychologist, Clinical Staff Psychologist, Business Consultant, and College Instructor at Henry Ford Community College, The Pennsylvania State University Pittsburgh Extension, Blue Ridge Community College and Mary Baldwin College Adult Community Learning Center. In addition to *Paint Yourself Healed*, Michal is the author of several books: *Narrow Gate Understanding Biblical Healing, Convinced By The Word Healed By God, Vessels of Power* and *Healing Leaves*, a manual on how to start and develop a healing outreach for the sick within the local church. Michal is both a guest lecturer and guest preacher.

Michal is an avid oil painting artist specializing in scenic America. She has painted and sold over 200 paintings. Her work has been on display in art galleries in Roanoke, VA, Gordonsville, VA and Staunton, VA.

Having grown up in Pennsylvania in a loving, devoutly Christian home with her parents and two older brothers, E. Michal Gayer currently lives in Virginia with her husband Robert. They have three grown sons Robbyn, Brett and Robert.

Contents

God's Word - God's Truth

"...who Himself bore our sins in His own body on the tree, that we, having died to sins, might live for righteousness — by whose stripes you were healed."

1 Peter 2:24

"...for He [God] Himself has said, I will not in any way fail you nor give you up nor leave you without support. [I will] not, [I will] not, [I will] not in any degree leave you helpless nor forsake nor let [you] down relax My hold on you)! [Assuredly not!]."

Hebrews 13:5 (AMP)

INTRODUCTION AND FOREWORD

Pot of Stew

When I first became sick, people were eager to bring meals to Bob and me. On one particular day, a large pot of stew, covered securely with a heavy lid, arrived. Later, many days into my healing, God used that pot of stew to bring fresh insight into my situation. He showed me that the heavy lid represented how closed off people can be to the deeper truths underlying Biblical healing and, in some ways, how closed off I had become as an evangelist.

Referring back to the day the stew arrived, I could see the pot on the stove warming, I could assume that I knew the ingredients that were in the pot, recall the taste of a good bowl of stew and even get excited about eating it. I knew enough about stew that I could have instructed others on how to make such a culinary delight. Segway in this analogy to Biblical healing. Now that serious illness had come upon me, I could see that my teachings on Biblical healing in the past were accurate, sound and valid, but they were from the closed perspective of a physically healthy person. Everything looks different when seen through the eyes of a seriously sick individual, especially when quality of life and life itself is threatened. The lid of traditional thinking, however, prevented the full depth of Biblical healing to emerge.

Extreme sickness calls for extreme measures. Go back to the stew for a moment. If you put a pot of stew on the stove to heat and allow it to get hot enough, it will begin to bubble and steam. I remember how the aroma filled the air as I lifted the lid that day. As we all know, steaming stew, bubbling in the pot, looks entirely different with the lid off than when we look at a closed pot. Now with the lid off, I could see the actual ingredients whereas before I could only think they were there and see them through the eyes of memory. As I stirred the meat, carrots and potatoes, the configuration of the stew changed with every stir. More aroma arose.

That stew, as you well know, would never do me any good to nourish my body unless I lifted the lid, stirred until it was ready and then partook. I can see now that when cataclysmic sickness comes, looking at Biblical healing from the point of view of only a well person just isn't enough. If I wanted to get well, I had to "take the lid off" my long-standing spiritual knowledge and concepts. In a sense, I had to be willing to "stir the soup" and let the Holy Spirit reorganize and rearrange my thinking into a better, more savory reality. Finally, I had to ladle out and "eat the stew" if I wanted to be nourished by it. In a similar manner, I had to actively participate with the power and movement of God to heal me in order for me to be healed by God.

This book will contain a narrative of how God took the lid off the stewpot of my life in order to position me rightly so I could receive my cure from an inoperable, incurable, cancerous brainstem tumor. The narrative will include numerous insights into Biblical healing and many revelations which I received while being healed. I believe this firsthand knowledge will be extremely helpful. It will also be a necessary reality check for some. As with any personal narrative, some of this material is highly unique to me and my circumstances and will not be applicable for everyone; however, the abundance of profound truths, insights and revelations that I received have the potential to move anyone in the right direction toward receiving total and complete healing from sickness or debility. We must be willing to lift the lid off all preconceived understandings, ideas and notions about Biblical healing and let God speak directly to our hearts concerning the uniqueness of our individual positions.

The title of this book, which is many steps away from the stew example I just gave, will be explained in future chapters. For now, I just want to entice you to lift the lid on your personal stewpot of life and let the Holy Spirit lead you to the place where you can "PAINT YOURSELF HEALED!"

Paint Yourself Healed

By E. Michal Gayer

Sickness has struck
  That blow severe,
Casting you down
  Into panic and fear.

You've hit the white wall,
  Weak, puny and pale;
It stares you down,
  Screaming, "Falter and fail."

Yet another voice,
  So calm and deep,
Says, "Take action now.
  It's too soon to sleep."

The Great Artist of Life
  Has given you skill.
Choose life! Do it now!
  Make firm your will.

With full bucket of Truth
  And grand brush of Power,
Action is needed
  To conquer this hour.

Decide right now
  His footsteps to follow.
Take your faith stand
  With no time to wallow!

Accept the challenge.
  Face your white wall.
"Follow me," He cries.
  Answer the call.

At Calvary's cross,
  Jesus' blood was shed.
So adjust your life.
  Paint that wall red!

Pick up God's brush,
  His power to wield.
Apply God's Truth
  and paint yourself healed!

CHAPTER ONE

PAINT YOURSELF HEALED!

Be a Doer (ref. James 1:23-24)

The joy of the Christmas season was still heavy in the air with the ringing in of the New Year. It burst forth with promise and excitement. My husband Bob and I were eager to use the fluffy, white down-comforter given to us as a Christmas gift. It was so soft, cuddly and comforting. Sleeping under this heavenly blanket would be a true luxury. Little did we know that fate was about to step in. In the course of three nights of sleeping under this gentle fluff, an allergic reaction began in my body. It started with mere itching of the eyes and developed quickly into severe vertigo, dizziness and loss of balance. Walking unassisted became impossible. I was immobilized! Something terrible had me in its grip!

Before we go any further, it might be helpful to share with you a little about our ministry so you can gain perspective as we move through this true-life story of healing, hope and personal spiritual growth. Bob and I have been in the healing ministry of Jesus Christ for well over 20 years ministering as Lightshine Ministries International. I have written three books, numerous manuals and DVD teachings in addition to being the main guest speaker (evangelist) in churches. With Bob arranging and doing all administrative aspects of the ministry, we have preached and ministered in nearly 600 churches from coast-to-coast in the United States, Canada and Mexico. In addition, we have distributed free Bibles and free Christian education materials into over 50 countries worldwide. Most of the teaching materials focused on Biblical healing. After creating and administering the Healing Rooms of Augusta County, VA for over thirteen years, we helped start dozens of healing ministries programs throughout Africa, Asia and points beyond. I thought I had it pretty much put together about understanding Biblical healing until that devastating sickness engulfed me early that January.

When it was apparent that I could not walk unaided, we knew we had to seek medical help. The first diagnosis at the walk-in-clinic was allergic reaction, congestion or sinusitis. All of these were attributed to the down comforter. When vertigo did not clear, I began being referred one-by-one to seven different doctors over a five-month's period. This included a General Physician, Ear, Nose and Throat specialist, several weeks' sessions of physical therapy at a local hospital, Gynecologist, Endocrinologist, Ophthalmologist and even a Cardiologist. The general opinion was that the vertigo was caused by some form of difficult to diagnose inner ear problem. I did the Epley maneuver and the Somersault ear realignment procedures to no avail. Things first began to clear when my Cardiologist insisted that I request having an MRI, magnetic resonance imaging evaluation, done as soon as possible. Upon his advice, I suggested this to my regular attending physician who followed through.

Shock can barely describe the crumbling of my world into fear and despair when the MRI results came in. Brain tumor!!! Not only a brain tumor but one of the worst kinds, very aggressive, located in the most critical part of my brain, the brain stem. The brain stem regulates automatic life support systems and functions. Our local hospital was unequipped to handle things like brain biopsies, brain neurosurgery, etc. so I was referred to a research oriented hospital about 50 miles from our home, the University of Virginia Hospital (UVA), Charlottesville, VA.

Everything moved at lightning speed. The MRI results came on a Friday and by the following Monday I had a 7:00 a.m.

appointment with the head of the Neuro-Oncology department followed several days later with a Lumbar Puncture, a 4 ½ hour Neuro-Ophthalmology exam and a meeting with a Neuro-Surgeon to arrange to have a brain biopsy. The results of the brain biopsy, had confirmed the diagnosis of an aggressively growing, inoperable cancerous tumor located on the brain stem. The report could not have been worse. In the doctor's opinion, I had several weeks or maybe a couple of months to live if there was no treatment. Soon followed a treatment plan to extend life but offered no medical cure. It included radiation therapy five days a week for six weeks and simultaneously chemotherapy and steroid therapy with at least half a dozen medications to counteract side-effects and prevent further illness.

Thousands of people were praying concerning this situation. Mostly they prayed that when the next MRI would be done that no cancer or tumor would be found. I was devastated when after all of that well-meant prayer had gone forth not only was there still a tumor, but I was told it had grown significantly since the first MRI. It appeared that the prayers simply did not accomplish the goal. My spiritual belief system was shaken to the core. How could that be after so many good people had prayed? The only conclusion I was forced to draw was that somehow, some way we as Christians were missing something, spiritually speaking, concerning appropriating God's healing power. The power to overcome this terrible attack upon my body simply was not there. Here is where I began to reevaluate every aspect of my spiritual belief system and here is where Bob and I entered an amazing journey of personal spiritual growth leading to healing.

The White Wall

I must introduce something important at this point. It may seem temporarily unrelated, but it is linked to the most profound essence of this book, the title...*Paint Yourself Healed - Healed by God of Brain Cancer*. I chose that title because it emphasizes the spiritual growth that we must seek to walk in, especially when overtaken by what looks like an impossible situation or when you feel like you hit a solid, immovable wall of insurmountable circumstances. Let me give you a simple illustration to help explain this better. Imagine that you are standing in a room facing a stark white wall. In your hand is a bucket of fire-engine red paint and in your other hand is a large paint brush. The object is to turn that white wall red. If you merely stand there holding these painting tools and not taking action, that white wall will never turn red. You can tell it to...you can pray for it to...you can hope it will, but it never will turn red until appropriate action is taken. Now, if instead of merely standing passively hoping, wishing and praying, you dip that brush into the paint and start brushing it on the white wall. Soon the white wall will begin to turn red. If you continue applying the paint, eventually there will no longer be a white wall but the glowing wall you painted red. The part of the book's title that says *"Paint Yourself Healed"* is to strongly suggest that you have a very real and important spiritual role to play in securing your healing. There are spiritual things that we grow into and apply in life in order for the healing promises of God to be fulfilled. Healing is so much more than just asking God to do it. As a matter of fact, there is little value in asking God to do what He has already done. The divine healing plan of God is already accomplished from His standpoint through the work of Jesus at the cross. Healing has been established. Now the work of appropriating that healing is our responsibility. Pick up your spiritual tools and *"Paint Yourself Healed."* Do your essential part. This cooperative venture with God is our responsibility and the rest of this book will focus upon entering that real-life journey which results in healing and restoration. I will share with you some of the amazing insights I have gained as God led me toward my healing victory.

Nineteen Severe Symptoms

Without question, I am not an advocate of bemoaning and recycling thoughts and complaints about one's symptoms, but I am going to mention a few of the nineteen debilitating symptoms I had during this time of sickness to reveal the magnitude of the healing that I received. The oncologist in charge of my case was very clear. There is no cure for the type of cancerous tumor that was lodged on my brain stem. The medical goal was to extend my life. Without treatment, I was living on borrowed time. With treatment, my life could be extended by months or possibly several years. The tumor was described as cancerous, inoperable, fast-growing, aggressive and having no cure. The medical situation was bleak at best.

The symptoms I experienced were debilitating. I could no longer walk without assistance due to dizziness and vertigo which accompanied me with every movement. Because of nystagmus my eyes constantly darted very rapidly back and forth, never stopping. Along with that, I had double vision seeing every object double. The people I looked at seemed to have four eyes, two noses and two mouths, etc. Riding in a car was a terrible experience because the oncoming traffic was doubled. Sometimes the second set of cars in my visual field would appear one on top of the other and sometimes alongside of each other. It always looked like we were headed for a collision or running off the road. Night time was worse with a blaze of headlights coming double at me in a continually disruptive array. There was also significant distortion in my vision with a loss of depth perception. No longer could I go up or down stairs because the stairs lacked visual depth looking like a solid slab just like the slide on a sliding board. Obviously driving a car or walking on my own was impossible. The tumor was mostly on the right side of the brain stem so I lost most of my hearing in the right ear and my facial muscles drooped significantly on the right side. The distortion of my face turned every smile into a grotesque grimace.

The condition I was in reduced me to sitting on the couch day after day. I could no longer see well enough to read, write, do calculations, work on the computer or do household chores. My favorite pleasures of playing the piano or working on an oil painting vanished as did the simple option to watch TV. Mostly I sat and stared or slept the days away. Unable to cook or clean house, all household functions rolled over to Bob. His caregiving obligation became enormous. Now he managed all household responsibilities, our ministry and two lives – his and mine. In addition, Bob accepted the task of taking me on the 50-mile trip to the UVA hospital and home again for six weeks of daily radiation treatments, additional hospital visits for MRIs and doctor's visits. Not only did Bob care for my physical needs, but he became a mainstay in my spiritual journey to health and wholeness praying and reading the Bible with me for several hours daily.

I would like to emphasize that three nationally acclaimed doctors of neuro-oncology, neuro-ophthalmology and neuro-surgery all agreed that my situation was incurable and while my symptoms might lesson slightly in severity, most likely they were permanent. Medically speaking the outcome for me was next to hopeless.

Unacceptable

As an Evangelist, I knew what the Bible teaches concerning healing. I had written three books with Biblical healing as the focus: *Narrow Gate Understanding Biblical Healing, Convinced by the Word Healed by God* and *Vessels of Power.* I had a good working knowledge of Biblical healing and knew, as a Christian, that divine healing is our legacy. The diagnosis given to me and the vast array of debilitating symptoms I was suffering could only be described in one word – UNACCEPTABLE! Bob and I immediately accepted the challenge of appropriating my born-again birthright of healing through faith in Jesus Christ and the Word of God. It happened this way. We received the bone-chilling knowledge that I had a brain tumor on a Friday. I was scheduled to preach at a church in Middletown, VA that Sunday. I fulfilled that commitment by the grace of God, but on Saturday, May 16, 2015 Bob and I sat in the parking lot of our motel and fashioned our prayer of agreement to receive healing from this dread disease. We stood on the truth of Matthew 18:19-20 where Jesus instructed saying, *"Again I say to you that if two of you agree on earth concerning anything that they ask, it will be done for them by My Father in heaven. For where two or three are gathered together in My name, I am there in the midst of them."* We talked, wept and prayed. Unbeknown to us we began a two-year spiritual journey that day which would lead to spiritual discovery, miracles and healing.

Disillusionment

Right off the start we ran into a discouraging experience. Looking back on it I am glad it happened because it set me on the right path toward healing. It just so happened that, without effort on my part, news of my situation spread rapidly. Soon thousands of people heard of my situation and were praying for me in large and small churches alike. Phone calls, cards and emails poured in. Roughly they conveyed the same message that someone was praying and wanted to assure me that the tumor was gone and would not appear on the next MRI. I was elated. A quick solution prayed through by numerous good Christian people was a welcome thought. The next MRI was done very soon after my primary diagnosis. When the results came in I've never felt more like the rug of life was jerked out from underneath my feet more severely than the day the doctor said, "The tumor has grown, gotten worse." How was that possible with thousands of people praying for the tumor to be gone? Not only was it not gone but it had grown worse! My emotions fell into deep despair while my spiritual belief system went into freefall. Either the people were not praying and were only giving lip service to me or their prayers were misguided and ineffectual. I decided on the latter and came abruptly to the realization that would ultimately save my life. It was this: if you are sick and in need of healing from God, it is your responsibility to develop a relationship with God that will bring healing results. Other people can assist in this process by prayer, ministry and support, but the appropriating of healing is primarily up to the sick person. Exceptions would be for children, the unconscious or those too sick or debilitated to respond, but for most of us, it is our responsibility to establish a healing relationship with God. The disillusionment and depression caused by believing what well-meaning folks were telling me, which proved to be incorrect information devoid of knowledge and power, at first set me back. It didn't take long though before Bob and I rallied into a commitment to seek God at a deeper more personal and more powerful level.

The Next Step

Having been raised in a devout Christian family and having served as a healing Evangelist for most of my adult life, the next step for us was obvious. We determined to fulfill all church related directives pertaining to healing like receiving the "laying on of hands, anointing with oil, the prayer of faith through the elders of the church, etc." It was our desire to respect the teachings of Jesus Christ and grow spiritually.

One thing I learned very soon was that things look different from the perspective of a sick person than a physically healthy one. Having preached and taught Biblical healing for over 20 years, I had a thorough grasp of Bible knowledge with a good understanding of Biblical healing. Those years, however, were spent teaching from the vantage point of someone in good health. Now that I was faced with a serious, life-threatening illness, the truths I had interpreted from the Bible took on unexpected nuances. Everything looked somewhat different. The fundamental structure remained the same, but the spiritual depth had changed. It was obvious that simple prayer might be all that is needed under the circumstances of common, lesser illnesses, but serious life-threatening diseases and debility require something more.

Quite frankly, as Christians in good standing in the church, we didn't know how to bring about the increase that was necessary to obtain healing results.

Holy Spirit Crash Course

One thing I knew for certain was that divine healing is real. I knew Jesus had made a way for me to appropriate the healing He won for me at the cross. All I had to do was "get it right" and "do it now without delay." Those words came to me as I sat up in bed unable to sleep. By morning it had become clear. I needed to refresh my thinking about spirituality and healing using the best resources I knew.

A few years before, I had preached a powerful sermon called "H-E-A-L" and now the Holy Spirit led me back to that teaching and the meanings attached to each letter. Even better He assigned four books, one to each letter. By sharing with you these titles I am not suggesting that everyone must read these specific books in order to be healed. It just so happens that these are excellent resources and have much to offer to any reader, but they were tailor-made to my need to grow into a deeper faith.

In my sermon, I had used the letter "H" of H-E-A-L to represent the first step in developing faith. Romans10:17 says "...faith comes by hearing, and hearing by the word of God." The letter "H" in H-E-A-L stands for "HEARING" and, as stated, is the first step in building faith. I had read the book *Healing the Sick* by T. L. Osborn before and found it thorough and comprehensive in discussing divine healing. Bob and I now reread the book together to refresh our minds on the basics of Biblical healing. We needed to bring this knowledge into our conscious awareness. It solidified the information we needed in order to move our current level of faith into a deeper, stronger framework.

After reading this book, which emphasized the important role of the Word of God in healing, I selected 77 key Scripture verses pertaining to healing and printed out sheets for easy reference. Bob and I read, prayed and meditated on portions of these verses daily for two years. We focused upon approximately 15 verses each day rotating them for variety and comprehensiveness. Working with these Scripture verses became the main bulwark of our prayer times and a key step toward building the faith we needed to appropriate healing. I believe that working and reworking these verses over and over again solidified my stand of faith and played an indisputable role in my eventual healing. (The 77 scripture verses that we used are printed at the back of this book.)

The letter "E" in H-E-A-L, as spoken in my sermon years before, stood for ENERGIZE. *Christ the Healer* by F.F. Bosworth was the second book we felt led to reread. It was a perfect fit emphasizing the fact that faith, born from hearing the Word of God, must become ENERGIZED to enable God's Word to shift from just being words on a page into inspirational truths. The Holy Spirit used this book to catapult us from "head knowledge" or "mental assent" into a deeper faith. Mental assent means a person agrees that the Word of God is true or factual, but they do not develop personal ownership or personalized meaning from it. Many Christians think they have strong faith because they believe in the truth of the Word of God, but their understanding of the Word is limited to mental assent. The difference between seeing only the natural reality of symptoms with debility and having sight into spiritual reality began to strongly emerge. From this came a shift in our spiritual meditation. We now took each healing Scripture and personalized it to my situation rewording it into a bold confession of faith. Every single day we proclaimed what we believed to be our personal truth as proclaimed in the Word of God. Our faith deepened. We began to see through spiritual eyes, looking intensely into how God reveals Himself to mankind. The need to view life from the spiritual perspective became clear with its vital importance very real to us now. No longer could we focus intensely on medical perspectives without true regard to the spiritual truths that infused them. This energizing process took faith to a new level. We were ready for the next step which came as we applied the essence of letter "A."

The letter "A" in H-E-A-L stood for ACTIVATE. The main idea comes from James 2:26 *"For as the body without the spirit is dead, so faith without works is dead also."* The book the Holy Spirit appropriately brought to attention was *How to Live and Not Die* by Norvel Hayes. The author emphasized the importance of a sick individual partnering actively with God. It was the very next step in developing power-filled faith. I soon realized that not only did I have a role to play in my healing, but it was a major role. The determination to secure healing is a key ingredient to receiving. Too many people take a passive stance ignoring scripture like Mark 11:22-24 in which Jesus admonishes us to *"speak to the mountain"* or Luke 10:19 which states *"Behold, I give you the authority to trample on serpents and scorpions, and over all the power of the enemy, and nothing shall by any means hurt you."* We are commanded to take authority over negative forces that attack our lives. Fighting back against sickness is crucial to being healed. To passively accept that sickness is going to destroy you, or cannot be cured, is to succumb to that inevitable destruction. The awareness that Bob and I had to take an aggressive stand locked in exactly when we needed it. Our prayer life changed dramatically at this point. We became aggressive condemning the sickness that came upon me and insisting in prayer that it leave. Our faith became very activated and our inner strength prospered. We moved seamlessly into the letter "L" in H-E-A-L!

Recalling the sermon I had preached on H-E-A-L, I was profoundly intrigued with the letter "L" which stood for LIBERATE. This disease had certainly imprisoned me. I was confined to a couch or chair and moved about only when someone assisted me. Looking back on the many months that I just sat not able to read, write, work the computer or even watch TV, I am more convinced than ever that without the empowerment of God, I could never have maintained such a life. To be liberated from the imprisonment of sickness was high on my list of needs. The book that I found most growth-producing and "liberating" was *The Life and Times of John G. Lake.* The book contains a collection of sermons by John G. Lake who is probably the most remarkable healing evangelist of the 20th century. He experienced thousands of miraculous healings in his ministry and evangelized throughout Africa. His teachings emphasize the need to weed one's "spiritual garden" of sin, surrender completely to God, anchor one's will toward God's will, win the battle between the spirit and the mind and take possession of one's healing as won at the cross by Jesus Christ. Deficiencies that block or stop the healing process exist in many areas and must be overcome. A conscious awareness of God's power "in" us and "for" us (Ephesians 1:19 AMP) emerged stronger than ever. The sense of God working within created a liberating environment. With a focus on God and His inward working, I gradually experienced a fresh alertness to the personal empowerment we have in Christ and a new determination to receive the fullness of healing which He died to give me. Freedom from sickness belonged to me through Jesus Christ!

All four of these books led me into a deeper understanding of Biblical healing and the development of a solid faith so necessary to appropriating healing. Relying on the letters H-E-A-L (Hearing, Energize, Activate and Liberate) helped me easily remember the progressive steps in the process of developing faith. By studying these words, my thinking was refreshed and a burning desire to gain victory over this thing was aroused in me. While there are other sources of enrichment, these particular books worked for Bob and me. They renewed our position on healing, helped us reach a deeper level of faith and inspired us to not only seek healing but go deeper into spiritual realities. I would have to say with certainty that acquiring sound Biblical knowledge about healing is absolutely necessary when seeking healing from a debilitating illness. How else can a person know that healing is the will of God without hearing it taught or proclaimed? How else would a person know that they should be an aggressive participant with God in their healing? How else would a person know the important role faith plays in receiving healing (Romans 10:14-15)? Knowledge about how to relate to God is necessary so a person can appropriately amend their thinking and their behavior to line up with the will of God.

I would strongly advise any sick person to acquire appropriate Biblical knowledge about healing. Such knowledge underlies the healing process and is crucial to developing faith to be healed.

Two Kinds of Prayer

In the course of rereading the four books just mentioned and developing a deeper faith, we became aware of two kinds of prayer both of which have their place in the healing process. PERSONALIZED PRAYER is the most familiar type of prayer. It is the kind of prayer most frequently heard from pulpits and at public events. It is also the most common type of prayer engaged in during private meditation. Personalized Prayer is simply talking things over with God. In essence it occurs when an individual talks "to" or "with" God regarding any circumstance or situation. On the other hand, when engaging in Power Prayer, the individual is not talking "to" or "with" God any more. The person involved in Power Praying is speaking "for" or on "behalf" of God as His representative or His voice directing God's power "against" or "into" a circumstance or situation.

The function of Personalized Prayer is mainly to build up the praying individual. It is an opportunity to acquire guidance and direction, receive emotional release, comfort, strength, support and similar kinds of growth oriented experiences. This kind of prayer is mostly for the person's own personal spiritual fellowship with God. Praise, worship and the renewing of one's intimate relationship with God frequently accompanies personalized times of prayer. This expressing of one's needs, love and devotion to God energizes the spiritual growth process. Where healing is concerned, it plays a significant role in setting the stage for Power Prayer.

Power Prayer

The main purpose of Power Prayer is for the person to assume the authority and dominion given them by Jesus Christ in order to act in His stead to distribute God's power into circumstances and situations here on earth. We have an important role to play in what happens especially where healing is concerned. We read about our authority given to us by Jesus Christ in Luke 10:19-20 where Jesus commands saying, *"I give you the authority to trample on serpents and scorpions, and over all the power of the enemy, and nothing shall by any means hurt you."* This verse and many others are telling us we have authority and we need to exercise it over devils, demons and sickness. Luke 9:1-2 states that Jesus called His twelve disciples together and *"...gave them power and authority over all demons, and to cure diseases. He sent them to preach the kingdom of God and to heal the sick."* Luke 10:8-9 further demonstrates the role of believers in healing where it indicates that Jesus sent 70 others out two-by-two and told them, *"Whatever city you enter...heal the sick there..."* Perhaps one of the most comprehensive directives to believers instructing them to be aware that negative forces must be authoritatively dealt with is found in Mark 11:22-24. This scripture reads, *"Have faith in God. For assuredly, I say to you, whoever says to this mountain, 'Be removed and be cast into the sea,' and does not doubt in his heart, but believes that those things he says will be done, he will have whatever he says, Therefore I say to you, whatever things you ask when you pray, believe that you receive them, and you will have them."* Jesus is directing our attention to the need to have power-filled faith when dealing with difficult circumstances and situations. He refers to the problems we face as "mountains" and instructs us to take action against them. Following His guidance, we speak with authority to those things and command constructive change. The admonition to "not doubt" the spiritual power of God, which follows our prayer efforts, reveals the depth of faith needed to accomplish Power Prayer.

In Power Praying you clearly see that the person commanding change is directing his speech toward the problem and not toward God. He is speaking to the "mountain," or problem, with strength and authority. It is taking the power God gave to believers (Luke 10:19-20) to wield through speech (Power Prayer) toward grievous circumstances to accomplish the will of God. The believer is God's representative, or His voice, directing power against or into any problem, circumstance or situation. The person speaks with authority "by faith" words that reflect God's will. When we speak words representing God's will, God's power accompanies them. That power flows. It impacts the situation that is being addressed to bring about God's will for corrective change, transformation and healing. In essence that is Power Prayer.

Power Prayer and Healing

It has always been God's long-range plan to live in people and have them partner with Him in such a way that His rule and reign is reestablished here on earth (Matthew 6:10, 2 Corinthians 6:16-17, John 17:23). There are other ways to accomplish this, but Power Prayer is one of the main ways to distribute God's power. Power Prayer plays an extremely important role in Biblical healing. Sickness is not from God. It is a work of the devil. Every sickness is an attack by the devil to bring loss, death and destruction to a person. In referencing the devil Jesus said, *"The thief does not come except to steal, and to kill, and to destroy. I have come that they may have life, and that they may have it more abundantly"* (John 10:10). With sickness being a tool of destruction by the devil, God worked out a remedy through Jesus Christ. It is God's will for people to be healed in this lifetime. The means for this to come about is through the great accomplishment of Jesus at the cross as stated in 1 Peter 2:24 which reads, *"Who Himself bore our sins in His own body on the tree, that we, having died to sins, might live for righteousness — **by whose stripes you were healed.**"* Healing was won for believers at the cross and now all that needs to be done is to appropriate that healing by faith. Power Praying is an important tool in the appropriating process. Properly applied along with Personalized Prayer, Power Praying will enable the will of God to be accomplished. Power Praying isn't just some extra option when serious illness strikes. It can become a life or death necessity.

Paint Yourself Healed

Convinced that I had an aggressive role to play in cooperating with God if I was going to receive the manifestation of my healing, a sense of personal spiritual empowerment grew. It developed alongside my newly sanctioned faith stance. This strength helped me understand why God had embedded this book's title so firmly in my mind. It wasn't just to have a catchy title. I truly was painting myself healed. I had picked up the brush of spirituality and was wielding it in Power Prayer and strong meditation. I refused to see myself sick even though I was seriously debilitated.

I cast off devils, spiritually cursed the cancerous tumor, commanded the departure of symptoms and directed the healing power of God throughout my body. I spoke to my "mountains" by faith and rooted myself in healing scripture all the while insisting that I was healed at the cross by the stripes Jesus took in my place (1 Peter 2:24). I painted myself healed, declared it and stood by that fact.

CHAPTER TWO

SPIRITUAL ALIGNMENT THE ROUTE TO HEALING

An Important Lesson Learned

When you have walked through the "valley of the shadow of death" and eventually emerged into God's bright sunlight of life, you will be forever changed! You will have learned some incredible lessons along the way. Under normal circumstances, a reasonable relationship with God and a few prayers might be enough, but if life introduces an extreme circumstance, it requires much more.

The moment I received the medical diagnosis of the condition that had come upon me, I was jerked into a new reality. The stark truth hit me like a cold splash of water on the face. That I had to have a working healing relationship with God was understood, but the fact that whether or not I was healed depended heavily upon me was unsettling. The depth and magnitude of this had never been realized by me before. It had been made medically very clear that the type of tumor that had attacked my brain was incurable and the best hope modern medicine could offer was the extension of my life for a period of time. Although I counted myself a good Christian, there was something earthshaking about the fact that if I was to be cured, it was strictly between God and me and nobody else. It was sobering to realize that others could help through prayer, support and ministry, but in the final analysis my healing would be strictly between God and me. I realized there were exceptions to this concerning young children, people too sick to function or people lacking ability, but for the vast majority of us it is a one-on-one journey between God and the sick person.

Once I got beyond this initial shock concerning the isolated spot I was in, I resolved to accept the challenge to form a workable healing relationship with God and determined to take whatever steps necessary to adjust my life completely to accommodate it. I determined that God and I were going to do this thing and then I leaned into it. After all, God has already provided everything that He is going to give us through Jesus Christ, His Word, the Holy Spirit and through His Universal Spiritual Principles. It was now my responsibility, just like it is for every sick individual, to appropriate healing from Him.

An Important Thought

Suddenly I became aware that it is possible for a real difference to exist between thinking you have it all right with God and actually having it correct and right. While I had a lifetime walk of faith, I discovered very soon, under the scrutiny of self-examination, that there were gaps and holes in some areas of my belief system. In some areas, I was rock solid strong, but in other areas I found myself full of unanswered questions. Bob and I began saturating ourselves deeper into the healing Word from the Bible. We read books by trusted authors, listened to numerous CDs, meditated and prayed investing two to three hours every day. I realize that how anyone chooses to seek God and fix spiritual weaknesses is an individual matter, but the urgency to do it is there. That being said, the very first important spiritual lesson I learned, as already stated, was that it was my responsibility to seek God for healing. I had to want it, believe that it was possible to receive it from Him, invest the effort that it takes and do the personal work necessary to appropriate my healing. This accepting of responsibility to actively participate with God was the **First Step** in the healing process.

Extracting Healing Life from the Word of God

It was obvious to me after many years of being a devoted Christian that the Word of God is our source for healing. Now under the stress of sickness, I held the Bible in front of me and realized afresh and anew that this wasn't just any book. It isn't just what we call the Old and New Testaments. It isn't just history. It isn't just chapters and verses. In my hands, I was holding the words which have the potential to connect me to God. When properly understood, the Word of God contains the very essence of God put down on paper in word form. It is the substance of truth. It is the Spirit of God in seed form. It is the reality of God expressed in soundbites. It is the power of God to heal, compressed and told in words. I recalled Psalm 107:20 which says, *"He (God) sent His Word and healed them..."* There is healing in the Word of God!

Now it takes determination to release the healing power of God from the Word. Of course, we must hear it and understand it. It is given to direct our lives, but we must allow the Word of God to change us. We are the ones that must crack it open and let God's truth and power move all over our lives. This takes time and effort, but when anyone works with the Word, the powerful essence of God becomes accessible.

That is why Proverbs 4:20-22 strongly instructs us to pay attention to God's Word. Listen to it. Keep it before our eyes and anchor it securely in our hearts because God's Words are containers packed full of life and full of health for those who thoroughly absorbed them.

And that is why Exodus 15:26 is so conditional. It is a Scripture verse loaded with revelation and promise. We see our responsibility right there in that verse which reads, *"If you diligently heed the voice of the Lord your God and do what is right in His sight, give ear to His commandments and keep all His statutes... I am the Lord who heals you."*

There is healing power contained in the Word of God. We need to not only hear and understand it, but break it open, work and rework it into our minds until the Word of God and we are in absolute agreement. If a person wants to be healed by God, they will need to be convinced by the Word that it is God's will and His commitment to heal them (Romans 4:21, 14:5). Bob and I took this very seriously. We made a little slogan and fervently spoke it saying that we were "Convinced by the Word! Healed by God!" Every day we would declare this slogan vigorously three or four times repeatedly. Each time we would beat the air with our fists to etch this into our minds. There is nothing curative from these gestures, but they worked to embolden the importance of the Word to us concerning healing. I am sure I will beat the air many times in my life shouting that "I am convinced by the Word! Healed by God!"

Clearing Up a Serious Misconception

Just like so many others, I had hoped that calling out to God would yield healing results after just one fervent prayer. Naturally I was disappointed when it didn't happen that way for me. It didn't take long before reality set in. Not everyone is healed after just one prayer, but everyone can be healed through the application of the Biblical healing principles of God. Let me put it this way. There are a number of ways that healing comes from God including through our immune system, medical intervention and various types of therapies. The Bible, however, reveals two main spiritual pathways to healing: (1) Spirit initiation and (2) those healings which come about through the proper application of Biblical principles.

Spirit initiation means the healing is initiated by God. These kinds of healings are frequently instantaneous and occasionally do not follow known Biblical principles. Sometimes people get confused when they hear that a person with little or no faith, with no relationship with Jesus, was prayed for and got healed. These healings are based on the sovereignty of God and His decision. This can mislead people into thinking that all healings following prayer should be instantaneous and don't require any input on our part. In all actuality, most healings are progressive and take place over a period of time after Biblical conditions are met.

The danger inherent in instantaneous healings is that if someone prays and doesn't receive instantaneously, they can become discouraged and give up. What we need to remember is that in the absence of an instantaneous, Spirit-initiated healing, God has made a sure way through which people can be healed. That way is through the application of Biblical principles as revealed in the Word of God.

Instantaneous healings are wonderful, but because they are rare, most of us will need to extract healing through the Word of God and faith. Drawing upon the Word of God to enable me to relate effectively to God's healing plan became **Step 2** in my healing journey.

Spiritual Alignment

The concept of spiritual alignment was not new to me, yet in the past I had never fully realized the depth of this phenomenon nor how important a role it plays in healing. Actually, spiritual alignment is one of the main components to Biblical Healing. It is born out of our relationship to the Word and was **Step 3** in my healing process. Let me explain a little.

First of all, we need to understand that healing from God is not haphazard. It follows a sure route. Spiritual alignment, it turns out, is the pathway along which God's healing power moves. Proper spiritual alignment means that all three of the basic components of a person, spirit, soul and body, are properly aligned with the Word of God and God's power can flow unimpeded within them. The specific order of authority for that power flow is from the spirit to the soul and from the soul into the physical body.

We as human beings were specifically created to live in two realms. We live in the natural environment of this world and, at the same time, we are to live in relationship with God, who is Spirit, in the spirit realm (John 4:24). To accomplish this dual citizenship, we have a spirit which enables us to relate to God and spiritual things. Likewise, we have a soul, which is our ability to think, feel, reason, make decisions and exercise our will. Our soul, for the most part, enables us to relate effectively to our natural surroundings. And, of course, we have a physical body which is the structure in which we live. When these features are operating optimally, a person can live in a manner pleasing to God in both the spirit realm and the natural realm.

Our spirit must come first in authority. It must be the ruling force in our lives since it is directly in contact with God. In your spirit is where Jesus and Father God have come to make their home with you (John 14:23) and where the Holy Spirit dwells (John 14:17). To receive healing from God, as based upon Biblical principles, the optimal situation is to have these three components of our being properly aligned in the specific order just given. Enabling the human spirit to exercise control over the soul is essential in securing effective spiritual alignment. The soul, subservient to the spirit, is now positioned to exercise control over the body. Following the will of God, the soul leads the body into godly behavior.

Our soul needs to be submitted to the authority of the spirit and then exercise control over the body. The mind, in a sense, is command central for the body. A soul in strong agreement with the Word of God will manage the body for behavior pleasing to God in accordance to His will. In order to accomplish this properly, the soul needs to be renewed on the Word of God and in agreement with the Word (Romans 12:1-2). Remember, your soul is how you think, feel, reason, make decisions and exercise your will. It can take time and much effort to develop the soul effectively.

I believe it is safe to say that all of us struggle with something at the soul level or how to think, what emotions are proper, how to make decisions or how to exercise our will. For me, the battle raged in my soul almost daily. It became a daily struggle to submit my mind to the Word of God and keep it subservient to the Spirit within me. Fears, worries, anxieties and things like that would attempt to overwhelm and draw me away from God's plan for my life. Never underestimate the intensity of the battle that rages in the mind of a sick person.

It is most likely there, within the soul realm, that healing will either be secured or lost. There is a good reason for this. It is because the soul is the gateway to the physical body. If that gateway becomes blocked, healing is impeded or stopped all together. Remember, we are talking about proper spiritual alignment and how healing from God flows first through the spirit, then the soul, and last of all into the body.

The Key

Your "will" is the key to making your soul obedient to your spirit. The fact of the matter is that God gave people "free will." He gave us the right to make choices and decisions. He will

not overpower, rescind or take away a person's "free will."
1 Corinthians 6:20 says your spirit and your body belong to God.
The working of the soul is your responsibility. Every person is
free to cooperate with God or not.

If, as an act of your will, you decide to discipline your soul to
cooperate with and be in submission to God, your soul will strive
to accomplish that. If you do not will yourself to be in submission
to God, most likely you will not win the faith-destroying battle
that rages in your soul. Proper spiritual alignment is crucial
and it is your responsibility to see that everything is set in good
working order. This is an act of your will. Your will is the key
to your soul. Remember, your soul, if properly aligned and
submitted to your spirit will rule properly over your body, where
most sickness and disease resides.

Healing from God passes first through your spirit, into your
soul and finally into your body. It moves in the order of spirit,
soul, and body (3 John 2). If God's power is obstructed as it
moves from your spirit to your soul, that hindrance could mean
that God's power never reaches your body. This is important and
explains why so many people are not healed. This also explains
why some people are powerfully prayed for and not healed. It
could be that they are blocked somewhere in their soul, how they
think, preventing the dynamic flow of God's power into their
body.

Not Properly Aligned

For most of us our soul, how we think, feel, reason and
exercise our will, is not properly aligned with our spirit nor is
it in harmony with God and His Word. All people inherited that
misaligned condition originally from Adam. In the garden of
Eden, Adam and Eve began life in proper spiritual alignment. But
after Adam yielded to the temptation of the serpent, sin gained

entrance into his life. Adam's disobedience caused a separation between his spirit and God's Spirit and tremendous spiritual misalignment took place. Romans 1:20-23 reveals the impact of sin on our soul. It says our thoughts became *"futile – useless, ineffectual, pointless."* It further indicates that man thought himself wise, but his heart became darkened. The deterioration of the soul was passed down to every naturally born person through all generations because all men have sinned (Romans 3:23).

Only through the sacrificial life, death and resurrection of Jesus Christ could mankind ever hope to be put into proper spiritual alignment again. Because of this, when a person is born-again, they are set right with God in their spirit and they have the potential to establish proper spiritual alignment once more. The problem today is that so many of us have become content living in the misalignment we were born into. We either do not know how important it is to have proper spiritual alignment or we have become complacent thinking that misalignment doesn't really matter. God does not require us to be perfect to heal us, but since proper spiritual alignment is the route that God's healing power follows, misalignment can slow down the healing process or block it altogether.

Many things can cause spiritual misalignment, but the most crucial factor is that of not absorbing the Word at a deep and meaningful level. We need to strive for proper spiritual alignment.

Why Is This So Important?

The existence of spiritual misalignment within a person is extremely important because it prevents the proper development of and application of faith. As you know, faith is the appropriating agent or the necessary ingredient that enables us to receive anything from God. Having faith in God to heal you is all-important.

In reference to God, Hebrews 11:6 is perfectly clear that *"...without faith it is impossible to please Him..."* This isn't about making God happy. It's about being in a place where you have met the requirements of God whereby you can receive salvation, healing and other blessings from Him.

Faith, trusting God and trusting the finished work of Jesus Christ at the cross, is the route to receiving healing through the application of Biblical principles. When Jesus took the whiplashes upon His back and died on the cross, He obtained salvation for all mankind, which includes being saved from the eternal destruction of sin and being healed.

Neither salvation from sin nor healing comes about automatically. Both need to be appropriated. Faith is the appropriating agent. It is that spiritual ingredient within a person that enables them to receive from God.

Faith is developed within us when we hear and embrace the full essence of God as presented to us through the Word of God. Romans 10:17 tells us that faith comes by hearing the Word of God. But understand this, faith is much more than mere knowledge about God. It is much more than just understanding the Word of God. It is a "spiritual experience," a "state of being," that exists within an individual when that person has embraced the Word of God as their own personal truth.

We all need to develop with certainty the spiritual truth that our healing was won for us at the cross by Jesus Christ (1 Peter 2:24). Likewise, we need to allow that truth to be so completely real that it gives birth to the "experience" of faith. When we act upon the faith that exists within us, it enables us to appropriate the healing that belongs to us as won at the cross.

From the Word of God, we become knowledgeable of the fact that Jesus took our sicknesses and infirmities at the cross.

The Word gives us the understanding that if Jesus bore away your sicknesses and mine, we don't need to bear them (Matthew 8:17). Faith developed from this truth is key to receiving Biblical healing.

The Battleground

While faith is the appropriating agent to receiving Biblical healing, we need to be aware of the fact that different diseases and physical maladies require different levels of faith. For example, a small cut on your arm will most likely heal without exercising any great deal of faith. Serious life-threatening disorders, however, require much more. Here is where proper spiritual alignment becomes so crucial. It is within the soul that faith destroying struggles are most likely to appear. The soul becomes the battleground where emotional factors, as well as demonic forces, attempt to gain control in order to kill, steal and destroy.

Fear, excessive anxiety, doubt, unbelief, discouragement, depression and similar negative thoughts and emotions can run rampant within an individual. The faith battle is on! If downtrodden emotions or satanic forces steal your faith, you no longer have the spiritual tool so vital and essential to enabling you to appropriate healing through faith in the Word of God. Without faith, you are out of proper spiritual alignment and the route to healing has been compromised, but if you maintain strong faith, and proper spiritual alignment, healing will come. God's Word never returns to Him void. It accomplishes what He sent it to accomplish (Isaiah 55:11). Healing will come because all the promises of God in Christ Jesus are *"… Yes, and in Him Amen…"* (2 Corinthians 1:20). Developing faith to receive healing was **Step 4** in me moving toward complete healing.

Fight Back to Gain the Victory

You might think that having faith is the final step and yet it isn't. When my healing was not instantaneous through prayer, the laying on of hands, the prayer of faith with the elders and similar actions, I was okay with that because I believed that it surely would come about in a few days. That was not the case for me. I had to strike a firm faith stance and maintain it for many months before the first positive results appeared, but come they did!

Absolutely certain that healing through Jesus Christ belonged to me, I quickly learned that I was in this faith battle for the long haul. It is ironic that the last sermon I delivered before being diagnosed was entitled "Fight Back to Gain the Victory."

Where God is concerned, it is always too soon to quit. Jesus secured your healing at the cross and God's Word is sure and trustworthy! A lot of sick folks, however, do not receive healing because they give up the battle, or they do nothing to grow in faith, or they fail to take any strong spiritual action, or they do not believe that it is God's will for them to be healed. We need to cooperate with God through His universal spiritual principals until the victory is won. Fighting back against sickness and debility with spiritual diligence became **Step 5** in my progress toward wellness.

Develop a Healing Mindset – Point 1

I am going to list the key points from that final sermon which I delivered before sickness struck because they are so vitally important. There will be four in all and each one is instructional about how to fight back to overcome sickness and disease.

The very first point (1) is that you must develop a healing

focused mindset. What you believe about whether or not you will overcome sickness is your mindset concerning healing. The nature of your beliefs, or your mindset, will set the course as to whether or not you will receive healing.

I've already explained that we have three major component parts, spirit, soul and body. Within the body, the brain, which is the seat of the mind, is the master organ that, under most normal circumstances, controls the physical body. For example, if your mind determines that you are thirsty, it instructs your body to move and get a drink. Likewise, if your mind determines that you are hungry, it instructs your body to make the appropriate moves toward eating. In a general kind of way, the mind controls the body.

As already mentioned, it is God's design for our human spirit ruled by the Holy Spirit, who indwells all believers, to maintain control over a properly renewed mind (Romans 12:2) and a subjugated body (Romans 8:13). Where sickness is concerned, the goal is to have our minds develop a mindset strongly anchored toward healing, according to the Word of God. To have this strong mindset toward healing requires that we understand some things about God's healing plan.

God let it be known through His Word that it is His desire for us to be healed. It is His will to heal us and He is capable to heal us. It is essential that we understand that because Hebrews 11:6 reminds us that it is by faith that we receive from God. If we do not understand that God is willing, able and capable to heal us, how could we ever begin to appeal in strong believing faith for God to do just that? What you believe about this is crucial. If you believe that God has made you sick or is keeping you sick for any reason, your mind will in effect stop the healing process. If you believe God is working toward your healing, your mind will positively affect the healing process.

Through Jesus We See God's Plan For Healing

Everything Jesus said and did revealed God's intent for mankind. John 6:36 clearly indicates Jesus saying, *"For I have come down from heaven not to do my own will but the will of Him who sent me."* Jesus is the perfect expression of God's will in action. So, what did He demonstrate specific to healing concerning God's will? Well, He healed the sick. Matthew 12:15 says that a great multitude followed Him, *"... He healed them all."* Luke 6:19 notes, *"... And the whole multitude sought to touch Him for power went out from Him and healed them all."* Jesus healed all and everyone who came to Him and He healed every kind of sickness and every kind of disease (Matthew 9:35). No sickness was too difficult or too far gone. By Jesus healing all who came to Him, He demonstrated that it is God's will to heal all.

In addition, Jesus sent out His disciples to heal the sick. Matthew 10:7-8 records Jesus' instruction, *"... as you go, preach, saying, 'The kingdom of heaven is at hand. Heal the sick, cleanse the lepers, raise the dead, cast out demons; freely you've received, freely give."* In Mark 16:18 we hear Jesus, referencing believers, saying, *"... They will lay hands on the sick, and they will recover."* By His actions, Jesus clearly showed that it is God's will to heal.

Sickness is Not from God

Furthermore, the Bible indicates that the origin of sickness is not from God. John 3:6 states, *"... The devil has sinned from the beginning. For this purpose, the son of God was manifested, that he might destroy the works of the devil."* Father God calls sickness "captivity" (Job 42:10). Jesus called sickness "bondage" (Luke 13:16). The Holy Spirit calls sickness "oppression" (Acts 10:38).

Jesus healed and made whole those who were being destroyed by the captivity, bondage and oppression of sickness and disease. He came that we might have life and have it more abundantly (John 10:10). If we are going to cooperate with God's healing plan, we must develop a mindset that is aligned with the plan of God. We must have a mindset that includes the knowledge that it is God's will to heal, that God has the power to heal and that sickness is not from God. We need to resist sickness and disease and will ourselves totally, spirit, soul and body, toward healing. Therefore, you must have a mindset to fight back and secure the healing that God has for you!

Become a Receiver – Point 2

The second point (2) I would like to make about fighting back in order to be healed is that we need to learn how to become a candidate to receive from God. We must become a receiver. Although God is a God of love, we've already noted that neither salvation nor healing come about automatically. We must appropriate both by actions on our part. We must actively receive Jesus in order to receive salvation and we must actively appropriate healing to be healed. A lot of people live under the misconception that when they are sick, all they need to do is pray and keep on praying asking God to heal them. They believe the rest is up to Him. That is far from Biblical truth.

It is true that all the promises of God are *"Yes and Amen"* in Christ (2 Corinthians 1:20), but almost all of the promises of God hinge upon us having a proper and right relationship with Him. For example, Proverbs 28:9, Isaiah 1:15-16 and Micah 3:4 all note how sin blocks prayer from being answered. If we hold within us any unforgiveness, bitterness, resentment, unbridled anger, unrepented sin or anything that is against the will of God, it can become a block to the flow of God's healing power in our lives. Many people engulfed in sin, stuck in unforgiveness and estranged from God simply are not in a position to receive from Him no matter how long and hard people pray for them. I am not saying that every person who is sick and has not been healed is necessarily engulfed in sin, disobedience and a flawed relationship with God. There are other reasons why people do not become healed, but what I am saying is that if we are sick and want to be healed by God, we need to examine our lives to be certain we are in a right relationship with Him and learn how to properly receive from Him.

Other Complexities to Becoming a Receiver

We receive great guidance in Mark 11:22-24 where Jesus states, *"Have faith in God. For assuredly I say to you whoever says to this mountain, 'be removed and be cast into the sea,' and does not doubt in his heart, but believes that those things he says will be done, he will have whatever he says. Therefore, I say to you, whatever things you ask when you pray, believe that you receive them, and you will have them."* Two important ingredients are mentioned in this passage referencing prayer and receiving from God. First, Jesus cautions us to have the kind of faith in God that eliminates doubt in our hearts. Secondly, He advises that right when we pray, we are to believe that we receive. Only properly formed faith will enable a person to pray in that manner.

People get derailed because they have not cultivated strong faith enabling them to live free of doubt when they turn to God in prayer. They get further side tracked when they fail to believe that something vital and important "of God" is happening right there in the moment they pray. In short, many people have not learned how to cultivate faith and receive from God.

One thing that frequently happens concerning sickness is

that people pray and ask God to heal them and then they "try" to believe that their sickness is gone. If symptoms persist, the person slips into thoughts of doubt and unbelief. Sometimes they enter mind games of trying harder and harder to believe that the sickness is gone when it is not. They probably do not realize that while instant healings do occur, most of the time people are healed over a period of time. During that time frame, the individual needs to take a strong stand of faith.

Believing Wrong

Mostly these problems occur because people are trying to believe for the wrong thing. They are trying to believe for an immediate change in the natural circumstances in their body when in reality their faith does not match that belief. Their focus instead needs to be upon having unwavering faith in God to fulfill His Word to them by healing them. We need to believe two things are happening concerning God right in the moment that we are praying. First of all, when we pray, we need to believe that we are spiritually connected to God who is able to respond to our needs. Secondly, we need to believe that God is actually responding to us, according to the His Word, right in the moment that we are praying. We do not need to believe that sickness is instantly, totally gone, when often it isn't. We cannot force God into time frames. If instant healing comes, you'll know it, but if it does not come, that does not mean that God isn't working toward an effective healing conclusion. We simply, but firmly, need to believe that the power of God has moved on our behalf right when we pray and is bringing about healing results.

If a person cannot pray believing in faith for total and instant healing, which most people cannot do, then pray in increments for continuous healing. It does absolutely no good to offer faithless prayers because they do not bring results. Every time you pray, believe that right then and there God's power has been appropriated. Believe that it has moved to destroy a certain amount of diseased or debilitated cells and that His power has caused a certain number of healthy cells to appear or be healed. Every time you pray, keep believing in that healing process. None of us know how many infusions of God's healing prayer power are necessary to complete the task, so pray fervently. Fervent and diligent prayer that believes something powerful is taking place because you are connected to the great power force, which is God, is what is needed. That is the kind of faith and prayer that brings the results which we want to eventually experience.

Now some people will tell you that it is wrong to pray more than once for healing because that indicates a lack of faith. I do not see it that way. I believe it is important to pray diligently (1 Thessalonians 5:17). Every time we pray, we need to believe that God is doing what only He can do and that He is doing it right then and there to bring about healing for our bodies. Believe in the eminent, powerful working of God in your body every time you pray even if symptoms persist. Remember, God is invisible and much of His working is neither seen nor felt. Trust God and do not let doubt and unbelief enter in. Persevere as long as necessary until the work is accomplished. Fight back against sickness and disease by becoming a receiver of God's healing power. Remember, *"... It is God who works in you both to will and to do for His good pleasure"* (Philippians 2:13).

Stay the Course – Point 3

If we are going to successfully fight back against sickness, we will have to fervently "stay the course." This would be point three (3) that I am discussing about fighting back against disease. How a person develops this kind of determination is highly individualistic, but I want to suggest that the process is heavily involved with knowing who you are "in Christ" and practicing the presence of the Holy Spirit. In other words, once a person becomes born-again, they need to know what their spiritual responsibilities are and what privileges belong to them.

Each of us needs to discover how to tap into the power of God. When that is properly in place, you will have the fervor and determination to "stay the course" no matter how difficult or long it may take. To be able to endure hardship is essential in overcoming sickness and disease. You may need to go through medical treatment, surgery, pain and discomfort before your healing is completed. I firmly believe that God has given medical knowledge and technology to mankind as an asset in the healing process.

Too many people, however, lose the battle by giving up too soon. They quit fighting against the sickness that has come upon them and it overtakes them. 2 Timothy 4:7 indicates that we do not win the race until we have finished the course. The one who wins the race must run the race to the end. By practicing the presence of the Holy Spirit and living by who we are "in Christ", the solid character that is essential for us to "stay the course" becomes built into us. If we are going to accomplish this growth process, we need to know the Word of God.

Understand that when the New Birth takes place within a person, that person is brought into powerful union with Jesus Christ. He has been born anew through the supernatural, inner spiritual renewal that takes place as a result of the sovereign, powerful work of God. This cleansing, quickening and renewing process is accomplished by the power of the Holy Spirit who now comes to live within the born-again believer.

Prior to Jesus' resurrection, the Holy Spirit only moved upon certain people to accomplish specific works, as during Old Testament times. After Jesus' resurrection and because Jesus dealt with sin at the cross, the Holy Spirit is now able to come to live in people who receive the "new birth." He takes up residence within the born-again individual to help that person grow more into the image of Jesus Christ. He works to build the character of Christ into that person during this lifetime, so when natural death comes, the Holy Spirit transports that person's spirit into eternity. The born-again believer is living in a new, power-filled reality.

We, as born-again believers, are privileged to be different from all of the people who lived prior to the resurrection of Jesus Christ. We are now living, breathing, power-filled, new spiritual creatures who carry the very life of God, the Holy Spirit, within our being. It is a good idea for each of us to daily remind ourselves "who we are in Christ" and consider the presence of the Holy Spirit living within us. Practicing the presence of God in our lives will enable us to do the things that God has ordained for us to do including surviving sickness and disease.

Consider This – Point 4

Point four **(4)** would be that we must create an internal atmosphere for healing and keep it! Consider this, if you have received Jesus Christ as your Savior and made Him Lord of your life, you are born-again. You have been redeemed. Your sin debt has been paid for at the cross by Jesus Christ. Your sins have been remitted. You have been set free from the power of sin. You now have right standing with God. Your fellowship with God is restored. You are a child of God. You are now a partaker of God's divine nature. And best yet, God Himself, in the form of the Holy Spirit, has come to live powerfully and permanently within you. He has come to make His home in you. Realize that it is your right and your responsibility now to fight back against sickness and disease. Learn how to fight back to gain the victory! When I was so desperately ill, regaining a strong focus on the above realities did not come easily for me. To keep myself focused, I decided there were three things I needed to develop: patience, endurance and perseverance. Daily I would say out loud, "I have patience, endurance and perseverance." I would follow that statement with my resolve, "I will not falter. I will not fail. I will not doubt. I will endure." It helped me to remind myself to fight the good fight of faith all the way to the end of the race where I would gain the prize. I gained it! I am healed!

CHAPTER THREE

MANY MIRACLES

Guardian Angels – Miracle #1

The events described in the first chapter of this book took place over the first month following my diagnosis of having an incurable, aggressive, fast-growing, life-threatening brain tumor. Many other medical and spiritual things were also happening during and after that time period.

I received the initial diagnosis on a Monday and by Wednesday of that same week I found myself lying on a gurney waiting to receive a lumbar puncture (spinal tap). Hearing the diagnosis had been scary enough and now the thought of having someone plunge a long needle into my spine to extract spinal fluid was exceedingly unnerving. Not only did the procedure itself bring tremendous stress, but for some reason there was a delay of over an hour from the time I was prepared for the procedure until the spinal tap actually took place. I had a lot of time to think and pray trying to gain a spiritual perspective and stress relief. Nothing seemed to be happening in my favor when suddenly I looked to my left and saw a very large, taller than normal figure. He was dressed in battle armor, holding a sword, and was standing at the head of my bedside. It looked like a bright gold outline of a person with a mostly transparent body.

Now I need to explain to you that I am extremely wary of anyone describing visions to me. Until this moment, I would have most likely discounted the appearance of an angel, but there he stood facing the door as if guarding me. I turned away and looked down toward my feet and there on the right side of my bed stood another extremely large figure appearing to be dressed in armor, holding a sword also looking toward the door as if guarding me. I immediately attributed what I was experiencing to angelic presences and inexplicably the "peace that passes all understanding" swept over me. The intensity of the calm and peace was like I have never experienced before. It remained throughout the waiting time and during the entire procedure. The presence of God with me was dynamically real and powerfully effective. I counted this experience as the first of many miracles I received during this healing process.

The results of the lumbar puncture came at me like a two-edge sword. On the one hand, they did not find cancer in my spinal fluid which was great; however, because the spinal fluid was clear of disease, that necessitated two more tests to determine the specific nature of this cancer.

The Search for Cancer in My Eyes

The initial MRI had already revealed a brain tumor, but proper treatment could not begin until the exact nature of this tumor was ascertained. The next step in the search was to look for cancer in my eyes, so the very next day following the lumbar puncture I submitted to a four and one-half hour Neuro-Ophthalmology exam. Compared to the lumbar puncture these tests were far less threatening. The examination was fatiguing but bearable. I must have had six or seven tests that day for depth perception, color differentiation, visual acuity, etc. They took photographic images of my eyes and measured vision every way imaginable. In the next few months I had several more of these extensive eye examinations. Once again, the results from this initial exam produced the good news that there was no cancer in my eyes; however, the alarming next step stared me in the face.

Brain Biopsy

Not having been able to determine through the lumbar puncture or the eye exam the type of cancer that was plaguing me meant the next step in the diagnostic process was a brain stem biopsy. It was explained to me that a three-inch incision would be made at the base of my skull. Skin would be pulled back on either side so a hole could be drilled into my skull about the size of a dime. The surgeon would carefully insert a long needle into the brainstem tumor to extract tissue from the tumor in order to analyze it. This would require a specialized MRI, while I was asleep, to enable the surgeon to thread the needle between existing neurological structures. If he was successful, there would be minimal damage to my brain due to the surgery; however, this procedure was extremely complex and intricate. Great surgical skill was necessary. There were no guarantees that the outcome would be good. The negative possibilities meant I could be severely brain-damaged and debilitated or even die during the procedure; however, the oncologist firmly explained that I really had no choice but to submit to this surgery since all future treatment hinged upon the results. Bob and I prayed considering everything and with trust in God, consented to doing the procedure.

We were pleased that the date for this surgery was set several weeks into the future as this gave us time to pray and further seek the Lord.

Brain Surgery – Miracle #2

Because the tumor was located on the brain stem, no brain surgery was possible to remove the tumor. To do so would have been fatal; however, I was surprised to learn that a brain needle biopsy was technically considered surgery even though it would in no way correct the problem. It seemed like a cruel twist of fate to have to submit to this procedure with no curative result. Needless to say, I was exceedingly unnerved at going through it.

June 23rd came all too quickly, but there I was at 5 o'clock in the morning being prepped for surgery at UVA hospital. Dressed in a special surgical inflatable warming suit I lay on the narrow bed in a very small pre-surgery room. With very little delay at least 20 people briefly came into my room to introduce themselves to me. This included the surgery team, anesthesiology team and nursing team. The last two people who came were the main surgery nurse and her nursing student named Michelle. Anxiety was mounting and I desperately desired to have someone come and pray with me. I asked the nurse if she knew if anyone on my surgery team was a Christian. She stammered and finally said that there may be someone, but she did not know who that would be. She and Michelle left moments before they wheeled me from the holding room into the operating room. The operating room was a very large room and it looked to me like there were at least 40 people at different sections of the room. I am thinking now that multiple surgeries were taking place at the same time. As I lay there in the final minutes before surgery, I felt a surge of anxiety mounting when suddenly the student nurse Michelle walked to my bedside, took my hand caressingly and simply said, "I am a Christian." No sooner had she spoken those words when the anesthesiologist arrived and gently pushed her aside. As he began preparations to anesthetize me, Michelle walked quickly around the bed to my other side and taking my hand said, "I am praying for you." I squeezed her hand and almost as soon as I said "thank you" the anesthetic ushered in unconsciousness. The last thing I knew before the anesthetic had taken hold was an incredible awareness of the presence of God through this young woman. Michelle's coming forward as she did renewed my confidence that God was working things out for me. An absence of fear and a deep sense of peace that God was taking care of me flooded into my last conscious thought. For this young girl to step forward into what was perhaps the most critical crisis in my entire life and bring God into my most desperate moment, I count as Miracle #2 in my healing journey.

Recovery

When I opened my eyes in the recovery room, Bob was by my side. In my still groggy state I told him about Michelle. As they wheeled my bed out of the recovery room and into the hall, there was Michelle. She came and took my hand and I was able to tell her how much it meant to me that she was praying for me and that she had the spiritual sensitivity to come to me in my moment of need. There was no real time to talk as the orderly moved my bed forward on route for the sixth floor. This experience coming as it did in my most desperate moment showed the presence of God moving powerfully on my behalf.

They kept me overnight in the hospital. During that time, I had the opportunity to minister to a bevy of nurses. Both my surgeon and my oncologist came to check on me and delivered some very difficult news. Following the surgery my symptoms had gotten severely worse. Everything appeared in double vision, sometimes triple, swinging wildly back and forth. My balance was so bad I couldn't even begin to stand or walk. The doctor's opinion was that this increase in symptomatology was due to the surgery and could be transient or permanent. In as gentle a manner as two doctors can muster, they spoke in agreement that most likely the symptoms would be permanent. I looked away from the eyes of the doctor toward the ceiling on the left side of the room. There I saw what looked like hundreds of people and I knew instantly that the room was full of Angels. A slight turn of my head to the other side of the room revealed hundreds more. In spite of this terrible news an incredible calm swept over me as Miracle #3 unfolded.

That supernatural peace in the eye of the storm remained with me and I vowed to have normal vision and normal balance again through Jesus Christ. The next day after consenting to have the tissue that was extracted from my brain donated for research, I was wheeled out of the hospital. As I stepped into the car from the wheel chair, a very jovial orderly encouraged me saying, "Remember this, you may have a brain tumor, but the tumor doesn't have you." I pondered those words as I prepared for the spiritual road ahead. With profound double vision, disabling vertigo, extreme dizziness, incredible balance problems and a very sore back of the head, Bob and I headed for home.

Once at home one of the very first things I started to do, and would continue to do for many months, was practice seeing again. I would stare at an object that appeared double and swinging wildly back and forth. While straining my eyes in an attempt to anchor the object in single, stable vision, I commanded my body to line up with my spiritual reality. I took the same aggressive stand about every symptom, commanding proper function believing it would come someday. That someday was many days away, but Bob and I remained diligent to speak to these mountains of disability by faith in God to heal me (Mark 11:22-24). Despite maintaining a persistent stance, over a year passed before I started to see positive results. Eventually, however, they came!

Preplanning

The course of medical treatment was finalized. I would receive radiation therapy five days a week for six weeks. Concurrent with that would be daily chemotherapy and daily steroid therapy. The radiation therapy would be done at the hospital and the other two therapies would consist of taking pills. A lot was happening very suddenly. As much as I was able, I joined with Bob in taking practical steps to adjust our lives prior to beginning these therapies. We decided to give the house a thorough cleaning and vowed to maintain it in a minimal kind of way by every day examining each room and attending to it so the work would never pileup. We made the decision to walk away from our standard routines and put our life, as we knew it, on hold. Normally Bob and I worked doing ministry work each day. We decided to cut back everywhere we could. We asked friends to not visit or phone us for the first week or so until we carved out a workable schedule. I emailed every significant person and alerted them to the fact that I would be out of email contact for a period of time. We stocked our pantry with food, prepared some freezer meals and appreciated meals friends brought. Each day required travel expenses. Because of the medical schedule, we had to eat in a restaurant for at least one meal daily. To accommodate these added expenses, we took the money that we had been saving for a vacation and re-allocated it to meet these needs. I had been the main teacher in our weekly Bible study. Knowing that fatigue was predicted to accompany my medical regime, I worked with our group members so that each member would take a turn at teaching for the duration of my treatment. This careful preplanning removed significant stress and provided a type of peace and security.

Healed of Long Standing Phobia - Miracle #3

In preparation for the first radiation treatment, a medical mask had to be created. The mask would be a plastic mold of my face perfectly formed to hold my head immovable. To construct this mask a sheet of moist, flexible mesh was fit over my face and pressed against my face to make a mold. The mold was allowed to dry and harden. Once dry it was a very close configuration of my face. It would be clamped down securely over my face for each radiation session.

The radiation machine was enormous. It filled most of a very large room. It looked ominous. I would have to lie down on a movable table, have my head pinned down immovable with the newly constructed face mask and then be slowly moved into this overwhelming machine. It required that I lay still without speaking or moving for about 45 minutes.

Of course, I was given medication to relax me; however, the fact that I was even able to attempt this medical procedure was an absolute miracle of God. Let me explain this. Many people have a fear of going into the narrow opening of the radiation machine, but in my case, I had an acute phobia of being pinned down. It came about quite by accident when I was six years old. My playmates and I were playing "cowboys." In our play time, there were "bad guys" and "good guys." We needed a helpless victim to tie to a tree and I volunteered. My friends securely bound me to the tree. Something distracted them and they ran off to play leaving me tied to the tree. I became seized with panic and started screaming frantically. Finally, my mother, hearing the commotion, came out and released me. No harm had been intended, but the experience left me with a severe phobia of being held fast or placed in confined quarters. It lasted throughout my life rearing its anxiety-provoking head many times.

I was irrationally afraid to have my face pinned down and my body moved into the radiation machine in spite of being given medicine to calm me. Being put to sleep was medically inadvisable. The therapists were exceptionally gentle with me, but I knew I had to go into this machine. Bob and I prayed that God would give me the strength, courage and peace to do this medical procedure and the miracle healing came.

I did the first radiation treatment using the calming medicine and then did not take it for the rest of the six weeks. God healed me of a very long-standing and intense phobia! Doing this treatment was definitely miraculous.

Calm – Miracle #4

The daily journey for radiation treatment was 50 miles one way. Bob and I made the most of it in two ways. The first way we prospered in these trips was to spend the time praying or talking about God as we drove to the hospital. Time just appeared to fly by unnoticed. No more than we started to pray than we were already arriving at our destination. Time just didn't seem to exist. The second thing we did was try to enjoy ourselves. Because of the distance involved, lunch out was necessary. The radiation therapist knew all the exciting restaurants in Charlottesville. Daily he would make a suggestion of a new and interesting eatery. In the course of the six weeks, we were able to sample at least thirty restaurants. The vacation money we had to use toward these new expenses turned into a daily mini-vacation in spite of the serious nature of our travels.

Our travels were serious. In addition to the daily radiation treatments, which lasted for six weeks, every three months I had another MRI. It was followed by an appointment with the oncologist. I was blessed with a caring and gentle doctor. His staff absorbed his kind manner and provided very professional and loving support. There were many MRIs with follow-up doctor visits during my 18 months' recovery. Each visit held the potential for incredible anxiety due to the imminent possibility of bad news. Here is where God provided in a miraculous way. The peace that passes all understanding that emanates from God was with us every single time we went to UVA whether it was for radiation, an MRI or a doctor's visit. At times, we heard difficult things and at other times encouraging news. Regardless of what was coming our way, peace prevailed throughout all 6 weeks of radiation treatment and beyond. We were in the secret place of the Most High covered with His feathers (Psalm 91). I will forever be thankful to God for providing calm through even the most difficult storm. To hear what we heard at times and remain calm is nothing short of miraculous! It was God working within us!

Financial Support – Miracle #5

We placed our lives in the hands of God for my healing and our life. Prior to this sickness, we had traveled all across the United States as evangelists. I was the principle speaker and was blessed to have preached in over 600 churches. Our livelihood was maintained by love honorariums given to us by the churches where we preached and ministered. When I became unable to travel, our income stopped abruptly.

The miracle is that God provided for us daily throughout the time of my healing by moving upon people to send love gifts to us. By cutting corners wherever we could and through the generous gifts of people, we were able to meet every financial obligation we had and at the same time maintain our ministry outreach. This miracle of provision took the stress out of not being able to earn an income. It enabled us to focus intensely on my healing. God had been very good to us through wonderful, caring people.

Miraculous Healing – Miracle #6

My healing from an incurable disease puts my entire healing and restoration in the category of miraculous. Almost every doctor we saw said essentially the same thing about the type of cancer that had attacked my brain stem. Without question, they declared that it was incurable and that the symptoms were permanent. Yet the fact is, today I live free from cancer and symptom free! Now I can walk independently, read, write, do computation, use the computer and pursue my former interests of playing the piano and oil painting. All of this was medically unexpected and to me miraculous. The medical treatment I received played a role in this healing, but it was God, through faithfulness to His Word, that elevated me from the diagnosis of incurable into the cured category! I am forever grateful.

The healing I obtained followed all the known healing principles of God as presented in the Bible. It was my responsibility to fulfill God's conditions for healing. I had to battle with my mind to overcome many obstacles to healing while at the same time staying determined to complete the course through the many long months that were necessary to appropriate this healing. The healing came about as Bob and I diligently exercised faith in God. The power and strength of God brought us through just as He promised in His Word. Perhaps the best part of this is that God does not play favorites. What He does for one He will do for another. It is my hope that by writing this book, people will realize what is required of them and learn how to appropriate healing through Jesus Christ. He took our diseases at the cross and makes healing available for all of us who will fulfill His conditions (Romans 2:11).

I also like the fact so carefully put forth by John G. Lake in the book *His Life, His Sermons, His Boldness of Faith* compiled by Gloria Copeland. He states that miracles are "…the discovery, utilization and application of spiritual laws and powers of which the material scientist knows nothing" (pages 377-378). He further explains that God exists in a miracle-working realm and miracles for God are commonplace. I guess I do not fully understand everything about miracles except I do know that when my healing far exceeded known medical expectations, my healing fell into the category of miraculous!

CHAPTER FOUR

SPECIAL INSIGHTS

About this Chapter

This chapter contains accounts of several loosely organized experiences which ultimately led to healing. The insights and experiences I am about to discuss are uniquely personal to me. Each one of these experiences played a serious role in my healing. We know that every person is different one from the other. While much can be extrapolated from these experiences, each one of us must search to discover his or her own route through the healing process. That being said, I believe that helpful information and directives will emerge for you, the reader, through the sharing of this information.

Paint Yourself Healed

From the time of diagnosis until my healing was manifested in the natural, I received many God-inspired insights. *Paint Yourself Healed,* as the title for a new book, was probably the first. When the thought came to me, I assumed this was because I was an oil painting artist in addition to being an evangelist. I had painted over 250 oil paintings, most of which were already sold. It wasn't long, however, that I realized that this title was "God given" and carried an important instruction.

Immediately following the brain biopsy, I was very debilitated, unable to walk on my own or see clearly with an additional array of about 17 other symptoms. It was a frantic and demoralizing time in my life. God had made it clear to me that healing was available through the great sacrifice of Jesus at the cross, but His Word also indicated that I had to participate vigorously in the process to appropriate it.

The steroid medication was radically affecting my sleep. For about three months I averaged three or four hours of sleep each night. This wakefulness was accompanied by extreme fatigue. The positive side of this was that it afforded me many hours to ponder and consider my situation. I examined the various symptoms I was having and decided that most of them I could do nothing about; however, I felt that perhaps there was something I could do to improve my vision.

Two days after coming home from having the biopsy I found myself tired but awake at 4:30 a.m. Frustrated and scared I made an effort to retrain my vision. The ophthalmology report indicated that there was nothing wrong with my eyes, but somewhere between the brain stem and the ophthalmic nerves confusion reigned, due to the tumor, which resulted in the double vision and nystagmus (vision swinging back-and-forth uncontrollably) that I was now experiencing.

In an effort to retrain my eyes, I would stare at an object attempting to develop a single vision focus. What I soon learned was that vision out of the left eye had more nystagmus than the right and the right eye tended to see double more than the left. Rotating my head either direction gave me the option of either wildly swinging vision from the left eye or double vision from the right with confusion in the middle.

I would look at an article and gradually move my head to the side. As soon as double vision started to dominate I would go back to where I saw this object better attempting to gain single focus. There was a very thin slice of vision for me to work with. While attempting to focus my eyes into single stable vision, I would speak to my brain stem following the advice of Jesus in

Mark 11:22-24 commanding it to send and receive the proper signals. I likewise commanded, in Jesus' name, that the neurological structures in my brain would respond appropriately. I would stare at the secondary image of double vision and command it to focus into single vision. This would go on for about 20 or 30 attempts before eye strain would force me to stop.

Night after night I would practice eye focus and control. This continued without success for many weeks when suddenly one night, my eyes drew together into one image. I was elated. It was possible to see a single image! The excitement was short-lived for as suddenly as the eyes drew into a single image, they moved back into double vision. I forced myself to reject the input of the Neuro-Ophthalmologist who strongly insisted the double vision with nystagmus was permanent. After about 5 months of my home spun version of eye retraining, single focus would come and last a few seconds. I was encouraged.

I kept trying to retrain my eyes for single, stable vision. It took fifteen months before I began having episodes of clear, single vision which lasted for several hours. The first time this happened, it came about almost unnoticed. Bob and I had watched a TV movie and unexpectedly I became aware that I had watched the entire movie with single vision! It took two more months of "speaking to the mountain" and prayer before I would have a full day of single vision.

The nystagmus that began with ferocious, continuous, rapid eye movement got slower and slower until now, 18 months later, I am free from both nystagmus and double vision. About the time the nystagmus began to slow, depth perception began to return. The stair case no longer looked like a swinging, double vision sliding board. I could now go up and down stairs as normal.

The healing of my vision, without a doubt, falls under Mark 11:22-24. As I persisted *"speaking to this mountain of vision deficiency"* refusing to doubt, what I requested came to pass. I believe every time I attempted to retrain my eyes, I was "painting" myself healed. Every time I spoke my healing confession, meditated on healing scriptures or uttered words of spiritual power over my body, I was "painting" myself healed. Every time I forced myself to imagine myself functioning perfectly again, I was "painting" myself healed! Each application of spiritual truth changed me from the dark tones of hopelessness and despair into the bright, glowing colors of hope and faith.

I now understand that this phrase "paint yourself healed," which eventually became the title of this book, meant I had to see myself improving, then improved and finally healed while actively participating with God to reach the final results. Applied paint changes the color of the thing that was painted. Painting oneself healed is to apply, through faith, God's Word to bring about a permanent change to the "color" or circumstances of one's situation. A coat of paint makes the object you painted look the way you want it. Painting oneself healed by faith harnesses one's mind toward a healing focus. Then add the appropriate faith actions and you are on the way to being what you want – Healed!

Discouraged

Early into my retraining regime and after several days of unsuccessful vision retraining, I felt like quitting. The task was overwhelming. One night in the midst of despair I had the following conversation with the Holy Spirit (that wee small voice we hear within ourselves). It went like this:

Michal: "Am I able to do this?"

Holy Spirit: "You decide. I am able to help you."

Michal: "I don't know."

Holy Spirit: "What is it you fear?"

Michal: "I am afraid to throw all of my eggs in one basket and then if it fails have the rug pulled out from under me. I am afraid that I will trust and fail to be healed. Then my belief system will crumble and fall apart."

Holy Spirit: "Maybe it needs to crumble. Maybe your belief system needs revision. Trust Truth. Trust God wherever it leads. You have two choices: (1) Let God have His way that He is leading, or (2) lose out entirely on God's way. I say choose God in whatever direction it goes and be at peace. Choose life or choose death. Choose God's way or choose being out of the will of God. It is a terrible thing to fall out of the will of God. Choose God. Choose God's way and nothing less. Right now, Michal, choose!"

Michal: "I choose God's way. I choose God wherever it leads. There is no other choice."

Today, many months later, as I look back at the scribbled almost illegible words I had penned that late night in June 2015, I am so glad at the choice I made. Why was it so difficult for me to fully trust God? The answer came a few days later.

Baby in the Crib

Right in the midst of praying I heard a baby screaming and calling frantically for its mother, "Mommy! Mommy!" I stopped praying abruptly and stared at what I now know was a vision.

I saw a two-year-old child in a hospital bed screaming for her mother and her mother didn't come. In the vision, I saw the very young and frail child look toward a glass panel to the left of her crib. The little girl saw her Mommy standing there briefly and then her Mommy was gone. The child jumped up and down screaming. Heavy sobs and screams followed with one desperate cry after another, "Mommy! Mommy!"

This heart-wrenching experience actually happened exactly like I just described. I was that two year old child. Because of a bout of Streptococcus, I had to be hospitalized. The severity of the disease required that I had to be put in isolation for 10 days. My parents were not permitted to visit me. One day my mother came to sneak a peek at me through the glass panel trying very hard not to let me see her, but her efforts failed. Thus followed the anguished cries of the two year old, "Mommy! Mommy!"

Now as I relived this experience, my stomach churned and terrible sobs ushered forth. God had just shown me where my broken trust began. As a two year old child, I had no awareness that I was in the hospital for my own good to be healed. All I knew was that the woman I loved, depended upon and trusted (Mommy) had left me. A fear of trust that was born in that moment along with a sense of abandonment trailed throughout my life.

As a child, I couldn't know that my mother agonized over my being sick and longed to be with me. I couldn't know that God was delivering me from the brink of death back to my loving parents. Afterward my mother told me that when I was released from the hospital I had weeks of terrible tantrums and nightmares. In spite of the fact that I was raised by very loving and caring parents, a sliver of doubt and mistrust was lodged deep within me and accompanied me throughout life.

Not only did God show me in this vision the root cause of mistrust, but in showing it to me and enabling me to relive it through the eyes of an adult, He healed me emotionally. This sense of mistrust was hindering the healing process. With it gone, I am now free to receive, or so I thought.

The Origin of My Current Disease

Like so many people, I was thrilled at being set free from a lifelong sense of mistrust and thought that was the end of it. There was more revelation to come. I do not believe that we must see the emotional root of every sickness that comes; however, God wanted me to see the cause of the sickness that had come upon me. In my early professional career I had worked as a psychologist, so I understood how important the mind/body connection is. I knew that it is possible for some sicknesses to be born out of an association to certain traumatic events in one's life. It has been suggested that where cancer is concerned you can sometimes look back over the last two or three years of a person's life and see the trauma that underlies this disease.

The abandonment experience of the "baby in the crib" had tentacles of insecurity that reached deep into my life. The episode already described where playmates tied me to a tree and then abandoned me played right into this insecurity. Other episodes surfaced from time to time but none so severe as that which happened a few years before cancer formed in my body. It was a traumatic incident that came upon me through mismanagement in the church I attended at that time. It affected my ministry work and it seriously affected me.

Because the occurrence of disruption came upon Bob's and my ministry, this event became tangled with my concept of how God should respond. The question of how could God let something so disruptive come upon me was one issue I had to deal with. Once again abandonment rose full force in my life, but this time the abandonment seemed to be from God. Looking back upon the situation with a clear mind, it is obvious that God never abandoned me. The mind, however, can twist and confuse things so they do not match reality. God now showed me the whole chain of events from age two until just a few years back and how they produced seeds for sickness and disease.

It was necessary for me to see these links in order to be able to trust God fully for my healing. Possessing healing inside of you, through inner knowledge of the Word and trust in God, is necessary. If you can't fully trust, you can't fully possess. As God showed me the root cause of this sickness, I became certain and sure of God's will to heal me. Jesus took this sickness on the cross on my behalf and now I could possess it fully. That belief, accompanied by actual possession, started to draw all of my life forces into healing. It drew upon the spiritual power within me to properly align me, spirit, soul and body, with God's healing principles. The knowledge and possession of healing enabled me to look beyond the symptoms, fears, emotions, thoughts and all other things that rose up against it. I could not have gotten to this point had I not seen the link between this sickness and past events in my life.

Not every sickness is as intricately woven as the one that came upon me; however, I do believe it can be very helpful in the healing process if a person knows what psychological and/or spiritual factors may have come together to cause their disease to take hold. Regardless, it is essential that a person possess (hold onto) and realize in a clear way that healing is happening once they are properly submitted to God.

Confusion

I was in the spiritual growth process early into this healing journey making progress developing faith and developing a sound prayer life. Along the way, it was necessary to have periodic MRIs. This created a prayer dilemma. I was commanding the tumor to leave my body and since the next MRI was still many days away, I didn't know how to pray. Was it still there or was it gone? I had no way of knowing until the next MRI would be done. Do I keep commanding it to go? It occurred to me that I don't want to stop commanding if it was still there. I meditated and prayed concerning this problem and the answer came. It finally occurred to me that I do not need to know if the tumor was gone or not. All I needed to know is that the healing power of God is active in me at the moment of prayer and I needed to keep that inner knowing going regardless of what was going on in the natural. The MRI would eventually reveal the status of the tumor, but until that happened and even afterward, I needed to stay in faith that the power of God was active in my body doing what only God can do. I decided that I would continue to pound my situation with appropriate prayer whether I knew the status of the tumor or not. My faith had to rest on God through Christ Jesus. Faith believes regardless of natural circumstances.

To help me keep that focus, and not concern myself with what I could not know (the status of the tumor), I developed a personal confession writing each statement on a 3x5 card with a bold marking pen. I ended up with at least 30 cards which I read daily. Here is a sample of the kinds of things I wanted to have fixed in my mind:

"The healing power of God is active in me to heal me.
The healing power of God is working in me.
I am being healed right now.
The power of God is destroying sickness in me.
The healing power of God is destroying the tumor if it is still in me.

> The healing power of God is cleansing my body of all sickness and disease.
> The healing power of God is healing all wounds that have come from this disease.
> The healing power of God is making me well.
> The healing power of God is making me whole.
> All of my life forces are pulling with God to bring about healing.
> All of my life forces are participating in my healing.
> All of my life forces are united with the healing power of God making me well."

By declaring these and other confessions, I was feeding correct spiritual thinking into my soul and building crucial faith. I was opening my soul (mind) to the spirit. By exercising faith, the manifestation of healing in my flesh was being drawn from my spirit, into my soul and into my body. By using 3x5 cards, I could renew my confession of faith while building stronger faith at the same time. Did I mention that I taped 3x5 cards all around my desk area and all over the refrigerator? I wanted to keep the Word of God in front of my mind all day long. According to Proverbs 4:20-22, keeping the Word of God foremost in your mind and heart brings life and health to your body. I wasn't about to miss out through the neglect of God's Word.

You may have noticed in reading my confession above that I did not quote scripture and verse. Instead, I extracted the essence of God's Word and put that on the 3x5 cards. Putting it into my own words made it more immediate and real to me. By personalizing the scripture to my needs, it helped me to anchor God's truth securely in my mind. It was also very important for me to experience God's Word as "present and active in the moment." It was extremely helpful to meditate that while Jesus healed me at the cross many years ago (1 Peter 2:24), God's power was working in me NOW at this very moment. I tried very hard to absorb the fact that God was actually healing me in the exact moment when I prayed.

The Train

A thought that tried to plague me was the thought that when I wasn't meditating and praying nothing was happening. Nothing could be further from the truth, but twisted thoughts come so easily when fear seeps in. One night at 3:00 a.m. I was struggling with this particular misconception when I heard a train off in the distance gradually approaching our area. At first the sound of the train was soft, but as it came closer, the sound grew louder and louder. For a minute or two it stayed quite loud and as it passed on, the sound grew softer and softer until I could no longer hear it.

The Holy Spirit used this as a teaching moment. It was one of those inward, silent times of insight that went like this. Think of the train like the power of God. The train was moving before I heard it and it continued to move even after I could no longer hear it. God's power is operating along God's predetermined track all the time. It is happening even before you become aware of it and it continues to operate even when you are not aware of it. God's power is working all the time. Just like the train at a distance, it may seem faint or even silent and then like the train coming near, it may crescendo into a roar only to fade back. There are times it may seem to recede out of our awareness, but just like the train, it is moving and doing what it was sent to do all of the time whether we are aware of it or not.

This analogy was very encouraging. No matter what we are experiencing or whether we have some kind of tangible experience or awareness of God, God's power is still with us who believe. It is "in" us and "for" us. Ephesians 1:19 (AMP) tells us that God's power is measureless, limitless and surpasses greatness. Amazing, it is just amazing!

Spiritual Eyes

One of the most important lessons I learned was that we must learn how to see with "spiritual eyes." My natural vision was sorely messed up. Severely distorted double vision, swinging back and forth due to nystagmus and lacking depth perception is a severe handicap. Although my eyes were capable of normal vision, the neurological malfunction rendered my vision fairly useless. In a spiritual sense, my vision was equally messed up in the very early stages of this disorder. I wanted to see progress, feel it, experience it. Although I knew God's Word, I wanted something concrete, tangible and physical to happen. When week after week those types of evidences did not come, I had to fight off frustration and discouragement. One day as I sat in bed unable to sleep I heard the words, "Spiritual eyes…you need spiritual eyes."

As I pondered this, insight came. Bob and I had read the book of Ephesians over and over. We actually read it seven times from the Amplified Bible consecutively because of the rich encouraging content. Each time we read it, we grew spiritually by leaps and bounds. I began to understand what it meant to have "spiritual eyes."

"Spiritual eyes" means a person has become so influenced by the Word of God and so thoroughly embraces the Word as their own personal truth, that they have a spiritual perspective on life. While they do not deny the natural world and all of its trappings, they are guided by God's spiritual truths. If there is a conflict between the two, the person who can see with spiritual eyes will always accept God's point of view over the natural one.

1 Peter 2:24 tells us that *"by Jesus' stripes you were healed."* To someone suffering great pain or debility this is so hard to grasp that it is almost laughable to them. Yet we know this is truth. How does a person reconcile having great sickness with the fact that by Jesus' stripes you are healed? This requires "spiritual eyes."

Let me explain it this way. At the cross Jesus attained salvation for all. When the word salvation is properly understood, it means being saved eternally from the penalty of sin and being healed. Because Jesus "took" and "bore" our sicknesses at the cross (Matthew 8:17), the intent was that we should not have to carry them. When sickness comes upon a person, that person, if they made Jesus Christ Lord of their life and their Savior, has the privilege to appropriate healing from God through His universal spiritual principles as found in the Bible.

To grasp this truth and apply it to one's life to obtain healing necessitates seeing through "spiritual eyes." This means the person looks beyond the pain, inconvenience and discomfort their body might be going through and sees deep into spiritual truth. They hold fast to the promises of the Word of God in spite of difficulties in their body. The truth of the Word of God is more important and more real than their situation in the natural. They "look" at God's Word and accept it as a greater truth than anything that might be to the contrary. Spiritual truth takes precedence over natural evidence.

At first in my debilitated state, it was very difficult to acknowledge that I was already healed, but when I examined God's truth closely, I began to see through "spiritual eyes." Jesus took the brain tumor and all other diseases when those whiplashes were struck upon His back. When He died crucified on the cross, He paid the sin debt of all mankind. The way was made clear for people like you and me to accept this great sacrifice as done on our behalf. As I began to see this, I knew that within the spirit realm, I was totally healed. That became mine when I was born-again. Now that I am born-again, every spiritual blessing has been given to me including the right to appropriate healing through Biblical principles. I just need to devotedly accept God's plan for healing and apply it diligently into my life. Realizing all of this was seeing through "spiritual eyes!" Now I could understand how I was healed by Jesus at the cross and still have symptoms of sickness in my body. It became obvious that I had spiritual work to do. I needed to appropriate the healing that Jesus won for me!

Relying on "spiritual sight," Bob and I chose to accept the Word of God above whatever I was experiencing in the natural. By Jesus' stripes I had been healed and every day that I commanded sickness out of my body and directed healing to come in, we believed that was exactly what was happening, regardless of how I felt. Making the decision to believe God's Word above how things looked in the natural was probably the most important decision I have ever made. Living it out was not always easy, but it certainly was achievable. We accepted the challenge, put forth the necessary effort and the result is that I am healed!

The Body

Developing spiritual sight has its challenges but none as complicated as communicating with the body. You will recall that we said spiritual alignment plays a significate role in Biblical healing. If we are to have proper spiritual alignment that will permit God's healing power to move unhindered, we need to have our spirit in control over our soul, how we think, feel, reason, will and make decisions. Our soul, that is strongly renewed on the Word of God, needs to operate in such a way as to keep the body under the rule of the will of God. The order of authority and communication for optimal functioning is spirit, soul and body, in that order.

As challenging as it is to put your spirit in control and to renew your soul on the Word of God, it is even a greater challenge to communicate with the flesh. To help us transfer what Jesus did for us that is in our spirit, through the soul and into our body we rely heavily upon our brain. The brain, as a thinking apparatus, is the connecting link between the soul and the body.

Healing from God moves first through our born-again spirit, through our renewed soul and last of all into the body. If a person's mind gets blocked in the soul realm, this becomes a problem for transferring from the spirit to the body. You really do need the input of a properly renewed mind. It plays a crucial role in this important transfer process (Romans 12:1-2).

I discovered that Jesus' instructions in Mark 11:22-24 to be the most effective way to communicate with the body. Daily, Bob and I would command sickness out of my various sense organs speaking to each as if it was a "mountain" that needed to move. We met the daily challenge by setting our "wills" to work through each and every barrier. We relied upon our will to maintain the diligence this required. As the will goes, so goes the soul. As the soul goes, so goes the body. Every day we would speak to various parts of my body commanding them to function properly, subdue themselves to the will of God and be healed.

I told my body to respond to God's healing power and the healing life of Jesus Christ. I spoke to my body to receive that which Jesus died for. Bob and I daily acknowledged that we are joint heirs with Jesus and that we are seated in heavenly places in Christ Jesus. I strongly encourage you to read the book of Ephesians from the Amplified Bible. It is rich with insight.

Speaking to and commanding my body to be free from sickness and healed by God was not a one-time event. Bob and I continued to pray and meditate at least two hours every day ordering my body to respond to God's will. Gradually my will and God's will became "one" and the results were impressive. Remember, 1 Corinthians 6:20 says our spirit and our body belong to God. Our soul, on the other hand, remains under the control of our will. God will not go against a person's will, but if we can line up our spirit, soul and body with the will of God, things can start happening at the cellular level. It requires effort on our part as well as patience, perseverance and endurance.

In essence, when we believe the Word of God explicitly, we are using our conscious cognitive resources (soul) combined with our spiritual resources to convince our body at the cellular level to cooperate with and receive God's healing power. It works!

Trusting God

One would think that after the amazing personal revelations God had provided that it would have been easy for me to trust Him thereafter. It was, most of the time; however, when symptoms would flare up, it became tough again. Romans 8:5-8 helps us understand why our thoughts and emotions make it so hard to trust God all the time. It states, *"For those who live according to the flesh set their minds on the things of the flesh, but those who live according to the Spirit, the things of the Spirit. For to be carnally minded is death, but to be spiritually minded is life and peace. Because the carnal mind is enmity against God; for it is not subject to the law of God, nor indeed can be. So then, those who are in the flesh cannot please God."* The carnal mind is the human mind minus God. It fights against God's truth wanting to follow the dictates of the flesh. It takes effort to turn it God's way. To assist me in this process I made a list of mini-confessions. Confession in this context does not mean confession of sin. It means statements of convictions or beliefs. Here are some of them:

Father God, I am trusting:
1. …that you are good.
2. I am trusting you to remove this tumor.
3. I am trusting you to annihilate all cancer in my body.
4. I am trusting you to remove all symptoms of sickness and debility.
5. I am trusting you to restore proper vision, hearing, balance and everything that was damaged.
6. I am trusting you to heal my brain stem and cerebellum.
7. I am trusting you to protect me absolutely through the treatment process.
8. I am trusting you to strengthen and uphold me.
9. I am trusting you for total and complete healing and restoration.
10. I am trusting you that this disease and any others will never come back on me again.
11. I am trusting you for total and absolute cure.
12. I am trusting you with my life!

By rehearsing these over and over, my weakened strength of trust became stronger and stronger. To further appreciate this process, I applied some logic to what I knew about God. I decided life splits between good and evil. By definition God is "good" and the devil is "evil." I believe we can all agree that goodness is beneficial, something to desire and seek after. Goodness is trustworthy. God is a spiritual phenomenon that we cannot fully understand; however, we know that He is "good" because of His benevolence toward individuals and mankind in general.

God is Spirit (John 4:24). In essence we are spirit (1 Corinthians 2:11). We must relate to God through our spirit to His Spirit. That means our human spirit needs to come into relationship with God's Holy Spirit (John 4:24). Since "spirit" is not of the "sense nature" (of our five natural senses), relating to God becomes a faith relationship (Hebrews 11:6). The only way we can relate to God, therefore, is by faith. Through absolute trust in the belief that God exists and through evidence in life's experiences that God is "good," we discover that God is the highest form of goodness and trustworthiness. It is easy to trust stable goodness; therefore, trusting God should not be difficult.

The way we can know God is through Jesus Christ who came to reveal God to people. Even though we cannot touch, feel, taste, smell, see or know God through our five senses, Jesus made it clear that we must learn how to trust this amazing God-phenomenon absolutely with our whole heart, body, soul and spirit. Developing trusting faith is of supreme importance.

Healing is one of God's universal spiritual principles. It is absolutely linked into goodness. Healing is good. God is tethered to all of His creation, but He has unique ties to people. One reason God heals is because He is compassionate toward mankind. He is benevolent (good) toward people. He has healing virtue or power and is willing to heal people, but they must come to Him in the "Spirit to spirit" faith relationship. That is the only way we can relate to God. This is a phenomenon of absolute trust and faith that surpasses evidence from our natural senses.

Universal Spiritual Principles

Since healing is one of God's universal spiritual principles, a few words about this will be helpful especially in connection with prayer. Earlier we talked about how vital it is to know God's will. Knowing God's will can seem like an intimidating task, but it is not as elusive as it first appears. Tucked within the Word of God are revelations of God's will through His universal spiritual principles or spiritual laws. We are accustomed to thinking in terms of natural law, but we also need to recognize God's spiritual laws which have been set in place by God to govern spiritual aspects of life. These spiritual laws or universal spiritual principles represent God's plan for life and righteous living.

Certain characteristics surround God's universal spiritual principles. First of all, they originate in the character, nature and moral fiber of God and are an exact representation of His will. Since they were established by God, they are unchangeable by man, world circumstances or events. God's spiritual principles operate all of the time, day and night with no variance. They are universal in that they apply to all people everywhere regardless of race, color, creed or national origin. They affect all human life whether a person knows about them or not, whether a person believes in them or not and whether a person likes them or not. All of God's universal spiritual principles are established as the standard for life and work in harmony toward good according to God's purposes (Romans 8:28). Obedience to God's universal spiritual principles is the will of God!

While God's universal spiritual principles are recorded in the Bible, NOT everything in the Bible reflects these universal truths. For example, when the devil speaks as recorded in the Bible, that is not God speaking and when wicked people speak, that also does not signify God. These things are written into the Bible for varying purposes, but they do not necessarily represent God's complete truth. Our task in reading the Bible is to sort through the various stories, histories, poetry and human thinking to discover God's absolute truth, His universal spiritual principles.

These principles are not difficult to spot because they have one important characteristic and that is this, they apply to all people. Some things in the Bible applied only to certain people like priests or kings and some things applied only to the people of the day the Bible was written in, but God's universal spiritual principles apply to all people throughout all the ages. To locate these in the Word of God, simply ask yourself one question when you read a Scripture passage. Ask, "Does what I read apply to all people everywhere?" When you come upon a statement of truth that applies to all people, you have discovered one of God's universal spiritual principles. They are numerous in the Word of God.

Power and Principles

Now we come to something of extreme importance concerning God's power. These principles supersede, surpass and exceed things in our natural world. Every universal spiritual principle of God links directly to God's power flow. Every universal spiritual principle of God is a power line to God. When a person applies one of these principles into their life, God's power moves on behalf of that person in fulfillment of the principle they applied. We could say God's power is released when a person obediently exercises God's spiritual principles. Listen carefully, since God's power moves in accordance with His spiritual principles, we must discover and use them in order to experience His power. Concerning praying, we need to learn how to adjust our prayers to coincide with God's power principles. God will never go against His will; therefore, we must learn how to pray in accordance with God's spiritual laws because they are the will of God.

To receive healing through God's Biblical principle requires that we learn how to step away from the control of our senses into a faith/spirit relationship with God. We need to learn how to look away from the natural realm into the supernatural. We get help in this area by looking at Jesus' pattern of healing. This encourages us to believe in and take the step of faith into absolutely trusting God to heal us. We cannot do this through our senses. We are out of our league there. This is one reason why nonbelievers are at such an extreme disadvantage. Through Jesus' sacrificial life and eventual death on the cross on behalf of mankind, He made the way for people to appropriate healing through God's universal spiritual principle of healing.

All of this exists in the spirit realm and must be grasped by faith. As we exercise faith in the finished work of Jesus at the cross it is possible to transfer healing from our spirit to our soul and finally into our body where most sickness and disease live. This is one of those times that we must perceive with "spiritual eyes" first and see the spiritual phenomenon that took place at the cross. Next, we must take hold of this truth by absolute trust and faith, believing in the goodness of God to heal us. All of this precedes healing which finally manifests in the body.

Now!

Once I caught on to the truth behind healing, it was not difficult to take the next step. It was the "now" step. In Mark 11:22-24, Jesus encourages us to believe God right at the moment that we were praying. In other words, our faith needs to be active right when we are praying and it must remain so even when we stop praying. Jesus said do not doubt. A lot of people will pray then begin to wonder if anything was happening or not thus nullifying the power that had begun. Our faith is to remain continuous before, during and after times of prayer.

I really connected with the concept of "**NOW**." Every time Bob and I would pray, we made the decision to believe that the power of God was moving right then and there. We would say things like:

> "God's power is healing me **now**.
> I have powerful faith right **now**.
> God's power is working in me right **now**.
> I drive sickness and disease out of my body right **now**.
> Tumor, leave my body **now**.
> Symptoms be gone from my body **now**.
> I receive healing through Jesus Christ right **now**.
> I am being healed right **now**, this very minute."

Did I have instant results? No and yes. The changes in my body from sickness and disease to health and wholeness came gradually over a period of time, but the moving of the power of God within me and the laying down of new healthy cells to replace diseased cells began right away when I prayed. Even when I did not see a change in my body, I believed that a change was taking place in me because of the working of the power of God in me right in the moment of prayer.

I believe it is extremely helpful to be consciously aware of the working power of God within one's body. We should develop an ongoing continuous awareness of the flow of God's power reminding ourselves that the life of God is moving within. Likewise, it is vitally important to direct that flow toward personal growth as well as healing for the body. This awareness will facilitate the entire process of healing. Since we are seated with Christ Jesus in heavenly places (Ephesians 2:6) and are joint heirs with Jesus Christ (Romans 8:17), we are members of God's miracle working realm. It is time to let our faith connect with these realities. As believers, the power of God is "**in**" us and "**for**" us (Ephesians 1:19) working on our behalf, provided we accept it by faith and do our part to receive it!

A Facilitating Friendship

Sometimes it is medically recommended to take strong medicine like chemotherapy to fight cancer. If after consulting with God, the decision is made to take the medicine, make friends with your medication. By that I mean that you will do your body no service if you are sending negative messages to your body every time you take the medication. For some people chemotherapy is very difficult to take because of the side effects like nausea and fatigue. Some of those people develop a mindset that they hate taking the medicine and dread every dose. Because taking medicine is so distasteful to them, they will say things like, "I hate taking that poison."

If you are calling your medicine "poison" or fussing in a negative manner every time you take it, you are sending your body a negative message. It is natural for the body to try to reject those things which you don't want. Instead of speaking negatively over your medicine, see it as your friend. Make this a cooperative venture. You have made the decision to take the medicine with the belief that it's going to help you, so make friends with your medication. Surround it with a very positive attitude that it is good and helpful for your healing.

Bob and I would pray laying hands on my chemotherapy pills speaking words of encouragement. I would make statements like: "I thank God for this medicine. This medicine is being used by God in the healing process. Chemotherapy is my friend. Chemotherapy kills cancer. Chemotherapy helps heal my body. I want to take this medicine." After speaking thus, I would swallow those pills and thank God for healing me.

If you believe God wants to heal you using medicine, you will want to create a positive mindset concerning it. Many people experience nausea as a side effect to taking medication for cancer, but I never had even one day of nausea throughout the several rounds of chemotherapy. I believe the positive stance I took had a lot to do with this.

CHAPTER FIVE

PARTNERING WITH GOD

The Concept of Partnering

A careful reading of the Bible reveals an awesome partnership between God and His people that is almost too wondrous to grasp. We pick up clues all the way back into the Old Testament where we read in Leviticus 26:12 God saying, *"I will walk among you and be your God, and you shall be My people"* and in the prophecy of Joel 2:28-29 which reads, *"And it shall come to pass afterward that I will pour out My Spirit on all flesh; your sons and your daughters shall prophesy, your old men shall dream dreams, your young men shall see visions. And also on My menservants and on My maidservants, I will pour out My Spirit in those days."* Actually, all the way back in time to the first man and woman in the Garden of Eden, the concept of God and man in partnership is revealed. God assigned the "tending and keeping" of the Garden of Eden to Adam, the first man. He also assigned to him the naming of animals and gave him certain instructions to follow. God's fellowship with mankind began in a partnership with man and God each having specific responsibilities to each other.

Jesus brought the concept of partnership further into our thinking when He stated that He and the Father would live "in" us as stated in John 14:23. He further emphasized as recorded in John 14:20, *"At that day you will know that I am in My Father, and you in Me and I in you."* Jesus made it clear that the Holy Spirit would dwell in Believers (John 14:17). The 17th chapter of John brings this reality to bold new heights with Jesus indicating that He and Father God would be "one" with us and live "in" us. Early Christian thought paralleled this. 2 Corinthians 6:16 states God as saying, *"I will dwell in them and walk among them. I will be their God, and they shall be My people."*

The concept of spiritual partnership takes on new importance where divine healing is concerned. It lifts and carries with it the idea that while God developed a sure path to healing through the life, death and resurrection of Jesus Christ, it becomes a practical reality only for those who appropriate it. Another way of saying it is that divine healing becomes a practical reality only for those who partner with God to receive it. The statement of James 4:3 *"You ask and do not receive, because you ask amiss, that you may spend it on your pleasures"* takes on chilling meaning. The unique reality of responsibility to "only believe" (Luke 8:50) and then "do" (James 1:25) according to God's will underlies healing theory.

When I first recognized that I had a role to play in the healing process, I felt overwhelmed by the question, "Could I do it?" But once I understood partnership, everything became workable and even comforting. God through Jesus Christ did the hard part for us, *"by Jesus' stripes you have been healed"* (1 Peter 2:24). All that remains is for the believer to become appropriately involved in meeting God's faith standard and become a recipient of what He has already provided. God has made possible that which man, on his own, could not do!

As with so many spiritual things, this is so much easier to articulate than to do, but the heartening part is that once a person decides and chooses God's path to healing, the Holy Spirit, who dwells within each believer, sets to work to make the conditions of God workable and doable. In other words, the sincere person who commits to Biblical healing gets help from God every step of the way.

In my growing-up process, I would swing between "good" days and "not so good days," but I discovered early that the Holy Spirit would accompany me through both with comfort, courage and spiritual strength on a day-by-day basis. He taught me how when having done all to stand (Ephesians 11:13), how to pray (Mark 11:22-24), how to rise out of emotional lows (Joel 3:10) and how to receive by faith (Hebrews 11th chapter). We "partnered" on the entire journey from sickness to health and wholeness. Hebrews 13:5 from the Amplified Bible was a mainstay for me. It reads, *"...for He [God] Himself has said, I will not in any way fail you nor give you up nor leave you without support. [I will] not, [I will] not, [I will] not in any degree leave you helpless nor forsake nor let [you] down (relax My hold on you)! [Assuredly not!]."* God's emphatic position of personal help expressly for me as I went through the *"valley of the shadow of death"* (Psalm 23), reassured and comforted me more than I can say. I learned how to not fear things that were out of my control because those exact things were under the control of God no matter what I was feeling at the moment.

God showed me that if I would pray according to His "will" and His Word, I would be speaking for Him. I would articulate the words, but God's power would travel with them to accomplish what was spoken. Therefore, it became easy for me to believe in the things I prayed for. Mark 11:22-24 became my reality. I would command "my mountains" to move, expect them to move and trust that eventually they would move. Did these things happen instantly for me? No, sometimes I had to bombard things within my situation many times over before change took place. If you had been sitting in the room listening to me command change in my body and see no result day after day, you might have thought this would be a fruitless venture; however, positive change eventually came and gradually symptoms lessened and left me completely. I don't understand the cellular functioning of the human body, but some things changed rather rapidly and others took many months; nonetheless, the symptoms diminished until they were gone.

Partnering with God resulted in my healing. It was necessary for me to take a fervent stance against sickness and disease, casting it out and commanding it to go. God did the work that only God can do and healed me.

Another Aspect of Partnership

While I believe that partnering with God is absolutely essential, there is another partnership that plays a crucial role in healing. That is the fellowship of believers. I was blessed with a group of strong Christians who stood with me in prayer and ministry throughout the duration of the healing process.

I stayed in email contact with these folks sending them a medical update every few months following each MRI. These updates helped my prayer partners to know specifically how to pray for me and it encouraged them at my progress. There were times when I hardly knew how to pray because the stress and frustration were so great. Knowing that people, whom I trusted, were praying for me gave me a great sense of comfort. Also, having this group of people standing with me in prayer created a kind of accountability for me. I had to press on not only for myself but for them as well. I am and always will be extremely grateful to those noble Christians who helped sustain me through my time of need.

Having a strong Christian family played an important role in my healing. They encouraged me and prayed for me. My husband, who not only took care of my physical needs, was a spiritual partner in the strongest sense. Having his courageous stand with me was a distinct and unique blessing. At low times, he would lift me up. When moments of deep discouragement and frustration would creep upon me, Bob refused to let me flounder or halt the fight. Having him pray with me daily, "out loud," was perhaps the single most important thing anyone could do for me. I emphasize the fact that we prayed together "out loud." By speaking "out loud" all of our prayers, our confessions of faith and our aggressive commands against the enemy's attack, our words became vehicles to strengthen and build up my faith. In many ways, it helped me have the patience I needed, the endurance that was required and the perseverance to press on to the goal.

While an individual can accomplish the healing journey alone, having people or even just one person to partner with them is incredibly helpful. I strongly recommend to sick individuals that they find two or three or more people that are willing to stand with them and help pray daily to completion of the healing. My family, the family of believers and Bob's spiritual partnership were key aspects to my healing. I lack adequate words to express how important this was to me and I will be eternally grateful.

1 Corinthians 12:26 points out that we are to reach out to each other. It reads, *"And if one member suffers, all the members suffer with it; or if one member is honored, all the members rejoice with it."* This is the true fellowship of believers. Our God is a God of partnership. He partners with us as individuals and His expectation is for believers to partner with each other as we go through life's trials and demands. I personally believe that every single church should be a healing center. Healing ministry programs should be established so no one has to travel through serious sickness alone. Bob and I had created and administrated the Healing Rooms of Augusta County, Virginia for 13 years prior to my getting sick. We learned that it is not difficult for a congregation to be organized in such a way as to meet the needs of the sick. Prayer teams can be established and one-on-

one arrangements can be made. It is not difficult. I believe this should happen in every Christian church. Healing was a main aspect of the ministry of Jesus Christ and, therefore, should be a main aspect of the modern Christian church.

Yes, to receive healing is an individual matter, but the ravages of sickness are so difficult to deal with that spiritual support is important to strengthening sick ones so they can take their strong stand of faith. If you were sick and standing before me right now, I would tell you to apply God's Word in your life, be patient, endure for as long as it takes, have perseverance, have faith in God and by all means acquire the mental mindset to PAINT YOURSELF HEALED and be healed of your infirmity!

Healing Scripture Verses

All Scripture is taken from the New King James Version of the Bible
unless otherwise indicated

1. **Proverbs 4:20-22** "My son, give attention to my words; Incline your ear to my sayings. Do not let them depart from your eyes; Keep them in the midst of your heart; for they are life to those who find them, and health to all their flesh."
2. **Joshua 21:45** "Not a word failed of any good thing which the LORD had spoken...All came to pass."
3. **Philippians 2:13** "...for it is God who works in you both to will and to do for His good pleasure."
4. **Romans 8:11** "...He who raised Christ from the dead will also give life to your mortal bodies through His Spirit who dwells in you."
5. **Exodus 15:26** "If you diligently heed the voice of the LORD your God and do what is right in His sight, give ear to His commandments and keep all His statutes, I will put (in the permissive sense) none of the diseases on you which I have brought on the Egyptians. For I am the LORD who heals you."
6. **Exodus 23:25** "So you shall serve the LORD your God, and He will bless your bread and your water. And I will take sickness away from the midst of you... I will fulfill the number of your days."
7. **Deuteronomy 7:15** "And the LORD will take away from you all sickness..."
8. **Psalm 103:3** "...Bless the LORD, who forgives all your iniquities, who heals all your diseases..."
9. **Psalm 107:20** "He sent His word and healed them, and delivered them from their destructions."

10. **Psalm 118:17** "I shall not die, but live, and declare the works of the LORD."

11. **Deuteronomy 30:19** "...I have set before you life and death, blessing and cursing...choose life."

12. **Jeremiah 30:17** "For I will restore health to you and heal you of your wounds..."

13. **Matthew 18:19-20** "...if two of you agree on earth concerning anything that they ask, it will be done for them by My Father in heaven. For where two or three are gathered together in My name, I am there in the midst of them."

14. **Mark 11:22-24** "Have faith in God. For assuredly, I say to you, whoever says to this mountain, 'Be removed and be cast into the sea,' and does not doubt in his heart, but believes that those things he says will be done, he will have whatever he says. Therefore I say to you, whatever things you ask when you pray, believe that you receive them, and you will have them."

15. **Mark 16:18** Believers, " will lay hands on the sick, and they will recover."

16. **John 10:10** "The thief does not come except to steal, and to kill, and to destroy. I have come that they may have life, and that they may have it more abundantly."

17. **Joel 3:10** "Let the weak say, 'I am strong.'"

18. **James 5:16** "...Is anyone among you sick? Let him call for the elders of the church, and let them pray over him, anointing him with oil in the name of the Lord. And the prayer of faith will save the sick, and the Lord will raise him up..."

19. **1 John 5:14-15** "Now this is the confidence that we have in Him, that if we ask anything according to His will, He hears us. And if we know that He hears us, whatever we ask, we know that we have the petitions that we have asked of Him."

20. **Mark 9:23** "Jesus said to him, "If you can believe, all things are possible to him who believes."

21. **Isaiah 41:10** "Fear not, for I am with you; be not dismayed, for I am your God. I will strengthen you, Yes, I will help you, I will uphold you with My righteous right hand."

22. **2 Tim 1:6** "For God has not given us a spirit of fear, but of power and of love and of a sound mind."

23. **Isaiah 54:17** "No weapon formed against you shall prosper, and every tongue which rises against you in judgment you shall condemn. This is the heritage of the servants of the LORD…"

24. **1 John 4:4** "You are of God, little children, and have overcome them, because He who is in you is greater than he who is in the world."

25. **Philippians 4:13** "I can do all things through Christ who strengthens me."

26. **Psalm 27:1** "The LORD is my light and my salvation; whom shall I fear? The LORD is the strength of my life…"

27. **1 Corinthians 6:20** "For you were bought at a price; therefore glorify God in your body and in your spirit, which are God's."

28. **Hebrews 10:23** "Let us hold fast the confession of our hope without wavering, for He who promised is faithful."

29. **Philippians 4:19** "And my God shall supply all your need according to His riches in glory by Christ Jesus."

30. **Galatians 2:20** "I have been crucified with Christ; it is no longer I who live, but Christ lives in me; and the life which I now live in the flesh I live by faith in the Son of God…"

31. **Colossians 1:27** "… Christ in you, the hope of glory."
32. **2 Corinthians 13:5** "Examine yourselves as to whether you are in the faith. Test yourselves. Do you not know yourselves, that Jesus Christ is in you?..."
33. **Jeremiah 33:3** "'Call to Me, and I will answer you...'"
34. **John 16:24** "Most assuredly, I say to you, whatever you ask the Father in My name He will give you…"
35. **Luke 10:19** "Behold, I give you the authority to trample on serpents and scorpions, and over all the power of the enemy, and nothing shall by any means hurt you."
36. **Luke 9:1-2** "Then He called His twelve disciples together and gave them power and authority over all demons, and to cure diseases. He sent them to preach the kingdom of God and to heal the sick."
37. **2 Peter 1:3-4** "…as His divine power has given to us all things that pertain to life and godliness, through the knowledge of Him…by which have been given to us exceedingly great and precious promises, that through these you may be partakers of the divine nature..."
38. **John 8:32** "And you shall know the truth, and the truth shall make you free."
39. **Hebrews 11:1** "Now faith is the substance of things hoped for, the evidence of things not seen. For by it the elders obtained a good testimony."
40. **Hebrews 11:6** "But without faith it is impossible to please Him, for he who comes to God must believe that He is, and that He is a rewarder of those who diligently seek Him."
41. **2 Cor 5:7-8** "For we walk by faith, not by sight."
42. **John 14:12-14** "Most assuredly, I say to you, he who believes in Me, the works that I do he will do also; and greater works than these he will do, because I go to My Father. And whatever you ask in My name, that I will do, that the Father may be glorified in the Son. If you ask anything in My name, I will do it."

43. **Romans 8:16-17** "The Spirit Himself bears witness with our spirit that we are children of God, and if children, then heirs — heirs of God and joint heirs with Christ..."
44. **Luke 1:37** "For with God nothing will be impossible."
45. **Matthew 17:20** "...if you have faith as a mustard seed, you will say to this mountain, 'Move from here to there,' and it will move; and nothing will be impossible for you."
46. **2 Corinthians 4:11** "...that the life of Jesus also may be manifested in our mortal flesh."
47. **Ephesians 5:30** "For we are members of His body, of His flesh and of His bones."
48. **James 2:20** "...faith without works is dead."
49. **John 6:63** "It is the Spirit who gives life...The words that I speak to you are spirit, and they are life."
50. **Romans 4:21** "...and being fully convinced that what He had promised He was also able to perform."
51. **Ezekiel 12:25** "For I am the LORD. I speak, and the word which I speak will come to pass..."
52. **Ezekiel 12:28** "...the word which I speak will be done, says the Lord GOD."
53. **Jeremiah 1:12** "Then the LORD said to me, "...I am ready to perform My word."
54. **1 Kings 8:56** "There has not failed one word of all His good promises..."
55. **Psalm 30:2** "O LORD my God, I cried out to You, and You healed me."
56. **Isaiah 53:5** "He was wounded for our transgressions, He was bruised for our iniquities; the chastisement for our peace was upon Him, and by His stripes we are healed."
57. **Matthew 8:17** "...that it might be fulfilled which was spoken by Isaiah the prophet, saying: "He Himself took our infirmities and bore our sicknesses.""

58. **1 Peter 2:24** "Who Himself bore our sins in His own body on the tree, that we, having died to sins, might live for righteousness — by whose stripes you were healed."

59. **John 15:7** "If you abide in Me, and My words abide in you, you will ask what you desire, and it shall be done for you..."

60. **Jeremiah 17:14** "Heal me, O LORD, and I shall be healed; save me, and I shall be saved, for You are my praise."

61. **Matthew 4:23** "And Jesus went about all Galilee, teaching in their synagogues, preaching the gospel of the kingdom, and healing all kinds of sickness and all kinds of disease among the people."

62. **Matthew 12:15** "And great multitudes followed Him, and He healed them all."

63. **Mathew 9:35** "Then Jesus went about all the cities and villages, teaching in their synagogues, preaching the gospel of the kingdom, and healing every sickness and every disease among the people."

64. **Luke 6:19** "And the whole multitude sought to touch Him, for power went out from Him and healed them all."

65. **Psalm 34:19** "Many are the afflictions of the righteous, but the LORD delivers him out of them all."

66. **James 4:7-8** "Therefore submit to God. Resist the devil and he will flee from you. Draw near to God and He will draw near to you."

67. **Matthew 7:13-14** "Enter by the narrow gate; for wide is the gate and broad is the way that leads to destruction, and there are many who go in by it. Because narrow is the gate and difficult is the way which leads to life, and there are few who find it."

68. **Psalm 91** "He who dwells in the secret place of the Most High shall abide under the shadow of the Almighty. I will say of the LORD, "He is my refuge and my fortress; My God, in Him I will trust." Surely He shall deliver you from the snare of the fowler and from the perilous pestilence. He shall cover you with His feathers, and under His wings you shall take refuge; His truth shall be your shield and buckler. You shall not be afraid of the terror by night, nor of the arrow that flies by day, nor of the pestilence that walks in darkness, nor of the destruction that lays waste at noonday. A thousand may fall at your side, and ten thousand at your right hand; but it shall not come near you. Only with your eyes shall you look, and see the reward of the wicked. Because you have made the LORD, who is my refuge, even the Most High, your dwelling place, No evil shall befall you, nor shall any plague come near your dwelling; For He shall give His angels charge over you, to keep you in all your ways. In their hands they shall bear you up, lest you dash your foot against a stone. You shall tread upon the lion and the cobra, the young lion and the serpent you shall trample underfoot. "Because he has set his love upon Me, therefore I will deliver him; I will set him on high, because he has known My name. He shall call upon Me, and I will answer him; I will be with him in trouble; I will deliver him and honor him. With long life I will satisfy him, and show him My salvation."

69. **Hebrews 13:5** "...for He [God] Himself has said, I will not in any way fail you nor give you up nor leave you without support. [I will] not, [I will] not, [I will] not in any degree leave you helpless nor forsake nor let [you] down (relax My hold on you)! [Assuredly not!]" AMP

70. **Hebrews 13:6** "The Lord is my Helper; I will not be seized with alarm [I will not fear or dread or be terrified..." AMP

71. **Hebrews 13:8** "Jesus Christ (the Messiah) is [always] the same, yesterday, today, [yes] and forever (to the ages)." AMP

72. **Hebrews 13:7** "Remember your leaders...and imitate their faith (their conviction that God exists and is the Creator and Ruler of all things, the Provider and Bestower of eternal salvation through Christ, and their leaning of the entire human personality on God in absolute trust and confidence in His **power**, **wisdom**, and **goodness**)." AMP

73. **Hebrews 4:12-13** "For the word of God is living and powerful, and sharper than any two-edged sword, piercing even to the division of soul and spirit, and of joints and marrow, and is a discerner of the thoughts and intents of the heart. And there is no creature hidden from His sight, but all things are naked and open to the eyes of Him to whom we must give account." NKJ

74. **Hebrews 4:12** "For the Word that God speaks is alive and full of power [making it active, operative, energizing, and effective]; it is sharper than any two-edged sword, penetrating to the dividing line of the breath of life (soul) and [the immortal] spirit, and of joints and marrow [of the deepest parts of our nature], exposing and sifting and analyzing and judging the very thoughts and purposes of the heart." AMP

75. **Acts 2:4** "And they were all filled (diffused throughout their souls) with the Holy Spirit..." AMP

76. **Psalm 23** "The LORD is my shepherd; I shall not want. He makes me to lie down in green pastures; He leads me beside the still waters. He restores my soul; He leads me in the paths of righteousness for His name's sake. Yea, though I walk through the valley of the shadow of death, I will fear no evil; for You are with me; Your rod and Your staff, they comfort me. You prepare a table before me in the presence of my enemies; You anoint my head with oil; My cup runs over. Surely goodness and mercy shall follow me all the days of my life; and I will dwell in the house of the LORD forever."

77. **Isaiah 55:11** "So shall My word be that goes forth from My mouth; It shall not return to Me void, but it shall accomplish what I please, and it shall prosper in the thing for which I sent it."